The Concept of Family

The Concept of Family

Morality, Individuation, and Reason
As Uniting Forces in Married Life

Paul Dennis Sporer

QUENSTEDT PRESS
AN IMPRINT OF
ANZA PUBLISHING

ANZA PUBLISHING, Chester, NY
Copyright © 2010 by Paul Dennis Sporer

Library of Congress Cataloguing-in-Publication Data
Sporer, Paul D.
  The concept of family / Paul Dennis Sporer.
      p. cm.
  Includes bibliographical references and index.
  ISBN 978-1-932490-39-8 (softcover : alk. paper)
  1. Families. 2. Families--Psychological aspects. 3.
Marriage--Psychological aspects. 4. Individuality. I.
Title.
  HQ734.S834 2010
  306.85--dc22   2010053257

Visit AnzaPublishing.com for more information on
outstanding authors and titles. Please support our efforts
to restore great literature to a place of prominence in
our culture.

ISBN-13: 978–1–932490–39–8 (softcover)

∞ This book is printed on acid-free paper.

To my dearest Cassandra

CONTENTS

True love is like seeing ghosts: We all talk about it, but few of us have ever seen one.

FRANÇOIS LA ROCHEFOUCAULD (1613-1680)

Love is an ideal thing, marriage a real thing; a confusion of the real with the ideal never goes unpunished.

JOHANN WOLFGANG VON GOETHE (1749-1862)

Chapter I

Introduction

Western civilisation has experienced great changes in the modern age, but the area that is probably the most misunderstood is that of the family. Not only have living patterns changed, but ideas and concepts about family life have also been modified. Nevertheless, the turbulence in one period of history should not make us blind to the fact that certain basic psychological factors, and associations of factors, never change in human nature. It is clear that the family of the 21st century is, *prima facie*, not so different in structure and activities from the family of 150 years earlier. Yet, equally as clearly, a man or woman of the past could hardly conform to the life patterns of a household of the present. Since the family is, for the vast majority of the human race, the most influential group in a person's early life, it must have substantial implications for that person's mental development, particularly those components of the mind that relate to individuality. In particular, the structure of the family is most important, since the collective definition of 'family' will invariably impact the organisation and functioning of the members of the household. In other words, the character of the whole affects the interaction of the parts. It is therefore undeniable, that changes in the interaction of family members potentially have a seriously negative effect not only on the residents of the household, but by extension, on larger society. For this reason we ask: What alterations have occurred to individual psychological functioning as a result of the shift in family structure from traditional to modern form?

Let us begin by stating a number of fundamentals. The family, in the most general context, consists of members connected by legal obligation and/or by genetics. This social unit might not hold any people who are married to each other, but might contain other persons related by varying degrees. Yet, in the narrowest sense, a family is ultimately based on the relationship between a husband and wife, as otherwise there could be no legal descendants from which to form these other types of blood relationships. For the marriage to be acceptable under customary precepts, the couple have a formal understanding or contract between them to undertake certain responsibilities for as long as the marriage exists. In European societies, this bond has further been sanctioned by the state laws pertaining to family, as the supervening communal authority recognises that a man and woman have entered a different 'mode' when they have made a public solemn promise of life-long mutual commitment and cooperation. Of course, men and women have other relationships which are not bound by any vow; these friendships can be formed or dissolved as either party pleases.

However, family is more than a simple grouping. In order for a person to become a viable marriage partner, he or she must possess a rich store of mental resources that should be contributed to the relationship for the benefit of both. Such traits cannot be derived from someone else, they must be obtained through independent development, an organic evolution of a personality. Thus, if a marriage is to function constructively, then both husband and wife must have fully developed personalities, each having acquired experience, knowledge, and wisdom. Such positive qualities must be integrated and attached to properly operating mental mechanisms. All of this can only be achieved when a person meets the challenges of life on their own, and deals with them in a manner that uses observation, reflection, and logic, engaging appropriate assistance when personal resources might be inadequate. We should understand that the development of character does not stop when a love relationship begins; the development must continue, and so both the man and woman must maintain a certain level of independence within the marriage, balanced by cooperation and solicitude.

Marriage is a unique type of relationship is unique precisely because it is founded upon a *concept of companionship* that two people jointly, with a similar vision, want to bring into reality. Each desires to experience a transformation of life by having a partner who will show consideration and respect. This transformation cannot be achieved through any other type of friendship or relationship. Hence, the concept of family is really an outgrowth of this concept of companionship.

Yet, at those points in married life where material matters 'take centre stage', there is a challenge to the continuing belief in the unique aspects of marriage, namely exclusivity in commitment, priority in attention, and continuing positive mutual dependence. It is up to the individual to determine which factors are primary, and which ones are secondary in perpetuating the relationship. The burden of success falls squarely on the shoulders of the individual. We can see, therefore, that managing the complexity of balancing material concerns with emotional needs requires maturity, discipline, objectivity, and good planning.

Of course, attaining the *apotheosis*, the perfect example, of any-thing requires diligent effort, and one cannot attain the 'ultimate' in different areas without balancing their effects. The effort to achieve important goals in life is meaningless unless it is energised by *spiritual transcendent* ideals, and in this case, the search for companionship must be driven by an *ideal of love*. Indeed, the most critical factor in connection with the intimate relationship is how the individual develops the ideal of love, which assists in formulat-ing appropriate rules that will provide gratification and affection within the structure of the family. This ideal's development must be viewed in its relation to the competing demands of other areas of life, and the mental and emotional aspects of the individual.

The 'just idealist' is that person who openly, fairly, assiduously seeks to bring to life what he envisions in his mind. For this indi-vidual, the marital relationship is an opportunity to become a bet-ter person, to move outside the mundane commonplace, to prog-ress above and beyond the present circumstances. Human beings naturally want to be loved, but the mature person who is devoted to justice wants also to give love in return. This cannot be accom-plished if there is weakness in character, ignorance, or incompe-tence. When we say that someone is dedicated to the ideal of love, this means that they desire affection and consideration from their intimate friendship, but they also want to give of themselves, so that the other person will equally benefit. In this way, the vision of a 'new self' can become a reality. Consequently, for a marriage to succeed as a viable medium for companionship, both partners must possess a strong, enthusiastic desire to continually experience the much sought-after qualities of respect, affection, admiration, and benevolence within the relationship.

Thus, in association with marriage and family, we have uncovered certain powerful ideas, which have been circulated and discussed in Western society for centuries. But these principles are not found in the conventions of our day. It is beyond debate that the concept of family at the beginning of the 21st century is not the same as it was at the beginning of the 19th century. Most people of the present-day do not see their own marriage as a unique relationship where ultimate contentment is to be found. In an individual's life, changes in psychology occur over years, with various aspects of character undergoing modification, but other aspects remaining the same. A similar pattern is found in collective psychology, although the changes are more likely to take decades or generations. We must therefore investigate which forces have been responsible for these changes in family life, and what attributes about marriage have remained essentially unaltered.

Sporer (2010C) reviews the history of marriage in the modern age, and the evidence shows that in the period after 1800 there was a gradual *retreat* from marriage, although the ideal remained untouched. Negative portrayals of marriage began to reach the average person, from books, magazines, newspapers, rumours, and gossip. As a result, many people developed a fear of married life, because they believed that the ideal of love would be damaged by the loss of affection from a husband or wife due to material concerns, business matters, or adultery. In order to reduce the likelihood of marrying the wrong person, the initial reaction was to *restrict* the circle of people that could be considered for marriage. By focussing on people within one's extended family as potential marriage partners, including close relations such as cousins, the vagaries of marrying a 'stranger' could be avoided. Although this brought a sense of security, it reduced opportunities that could only come by contact with people in larger society. It also put people into a more circumscribed world where challenges were reduced, and so character-building became stunted. Because people were limiting the individuation process, even marrying someone known well to the family, who had an attachment to moral and ethical principles, could not guarantee happiness in marriage and a resistance to temptations.

Women especially have used during the modern age of instability various devices to remove themselves from consideration for marriage; others found ways to delay marriage, at least until they felt mature enough to endure the problems that they feared would arise. By the late 19th century, society began to provide a means of establishing control in the household. Women became more confident about marriage when they realised that they could expand their independence by reducing fertility in order both to increase their free time, and to give more time to each child.

What we see in these patterns is that, in general, when there is an enlargement of concerns about an area of life, people ultimately narrow their focus, and fall back on plain materialism, in other words, *pragmatism*—a word that can carry both positive or negative connotations. The area of family is no exception. The 'just idealist' attempts to find, in everyday life, a balance between his own goals and desires and that of his spouse. We can see that the intelligent, resourceful individual seeks the greatest returns from an intimate relationship (companionship, affection, cooperation, reliance), as well as from social status (knowledge, autonomy, confidence, facility). However, if we agree that the integration of love with independence is superior to possessing only social status, then we must use the term pragmatism in the negative sense, which entails a *modification or rejection of ideals*; in our world, the focus currently is on methods that primarily preserve one's *independence*, not on methods that lead to genuine companionship. There are many external factors, with which the individual must contend, that seriously affect the desire for love and affection, and so, perhaps apprehensively, people learn to have their love ideal co-exist with their material aims. Then they learn to adjust, if possible, their relationships so that they will conform to the demands of a modern 'independent' lifestyle.

Thus, as it became difficult to objectively gauge gratification in the emotional sphere, psychological factors were over time subordinated to material issues, and numbers and figures—whether income, children, social level—arose as the tangible indicators of 'satisfaction' and 'success'. In the modern period, this pragmatism translates to a 'lifestyle' where the average man or woman lives in a family where the option exists for both husband and wife to work, where children are born at the time desired, the number of children are limited to a desired number, and the option exists to end the marriage if emotional satisfaction is not achieved. Nonetheless, what works in theory, 'on paper' so to speak, often does not work out in reality, if the theory is based on incorrect assumptions.

However, as researchers discovered in the 20th century, external indicators of happiness are not necessarily in accord with true emotional fulfilment. A person might appear 'happy' by society's criteria, but he might in fact be quite the opposite, a situation that few people can appreciate if they reflexively use material factors in their evaluations. How then does a person achieve happiness and contentment in relationships, if society cannot help him to see what is really important in life? The modern person must develop the capacity to know his internal needs, assess his own emotions and reactions clearly, to know his limitations and strengths. He must be able to put a mirror to his soul, to gain critical knowledge about the changes being made to his psyche by the social 'atmosphere'.

From observation, it is apparent that people regularly and frequently take into account their personal needs, which are to an extent modified by exogenous factors. Self-awareness, meaning having special, certain knowledge and cognisance of one's own personality and individuality, is a critical aspect in evaluation, as no person can find contentment unless they know their own desires. But we should not confuse this with selfishness. Indeed, self-awareness entails having the courage to move beyond subjectivity, so that distinctions between self-interest and other-interest can be operationalised. Nevertheless, it is not easy for even the most competent person to completely eliminate subjective perceptions. Humans, because they covet self-realisation, recognition, appreciation, and equal treatment, predicate their attraction to the opposite sex on, at the very least, a desire for security, material progress, and success in society. Self-interest can often be veiled by thoughts and expressions of love, and the result is that the desire for companionship is developed solely within the confines of the present social environment, with no attempt to move beyond the *status quo*. A person in such a situation must perforce have an extremely limited conception of love, since the refined and cultivated ideas about the subject contained in history and fiction, as found in stories, anecdotes, legends, and books, are not utilised to provide a broader vision. This inability to see life in its proper perspective inevitably produces false evaluations.

Thus, in order to ascertain the willingness and capability of the average person to establish and maintain a genuine companionate relationship, we need to examine the *reasoning mechanisms* that are used to develop and balance the various issues relating to the social form in which such a relationship will take, that of marriage and family. Invariably, reasoning mechanisms must be devoted to specifically producing viable moral principles. One might think that morality applies only to larger groups, but this is not true. Correct behaviour in any social environment depends on the mature use of moral precepts; indeed, morality, as a general theme, is a set of codes that governs social interaction. When we say a person uses 'moral reasoning', we are indicating that the person should engage in an objective interpretation of the needs, condition, motivations, or status of others. These capabilities of interpretation must be developed at home, within the 'mini-society' of the family household, before they can effectively be utilised in the outher world. Indeed, the most satisfying relationship comprises people who are utilising moral principles within the context of the 'group of two'. Hence, a concept of family arises before a concept of community. We can see that the astute person realises that it ultimately makes no sense to denigrate or compromise those actions which represent the greatness of human achievement, as these qualities can be experienced not only in marriage, but in broader society. Accordingly, there is the need for a thoroughgoing morality that does not discriminate between different situations using the predetermined social 'weight' of a group or its members as a basis. Even though marriage, in its outward manifestation, is 'played out' against a background of social considerations, the psychological aspects that determine correct moral action always remain paramount.

Because of the difficulty in implementing moral principles, an extended period of time must be allotted for conceptualisation and the preparation and gathering of resources. As a result, the construction of standards that lead to the 'excellent' or 'perfect' relationship commences sometime during childhood, probably between the ages of 7 and 10. During this period, certain factors affect the development of these standards. The conflict between continuing reliance on parents and the desire for independence creates insecurity, and the individual moves beyond the concept of the simple friendship. Children come to realise, albeit slowly, that they need more than just a causal acquaintance, but a real friend with whom they can form a dependable alliance. As they enter puberty, they have the understanding that their closest friend can only be someone from the opposite sex, and so the beginning of the lifelong desire for affiliation with the opposite sex. Boys and girls come to the realisation of the existence of a *special* bond between the masculine and feminine, and there is a growing understanding of the *timelessness* of such a connection. Because of this, examples that can be used to foster an ideal of love come first from family situations; patterns of behaviour which illustrate independence are drawn from social contexts. Hence, during the time spent within the family of origin, the ideal of love is cultivated against a background of uncertainty and instability in sex roles which can create insecurity. This uneasiness, within a well-integrated family, can actually lead to a better understanding of the processes that affect the interaction between men and women.

The various aspects of an ideal friendship become more solidified in adolescence, but unfortunately, in our day, this process has, for certain complex reasons, been stultified. Instead of showing some haste in becoming aware of what exactly constitutes 'love', that is, the actual, genuine day-to-day markers and signals, there is a tendency to add to one's knowledge but slowly. Perhaps this happens because they have come to understand that the profundity of the ideal makes its fulfilment elusive, and relationships therefore present no urgency to augment awareness. It is then a simple matter for the individual to put off crystallising the ideal, since it becomes increasingly apparent that it will not be reached except through great effort. Without assistance from family and adults, the ideal is left in pieces, immature and unintegrated.

When the children of our day are left to their own devices in determining the parameters of love and affection, without substantive support from family, they encounter many problems, not necessarily because they lack the potential to do it themselves, but rather due to the fact that they are surprisingly *slow to develop moral reasoning mechanisms*. Eisenberg et al. (1991) queried the attitudes of three groups of middle class children. One group of 32 children were tested a total of seven times as they progressed through the ages of 4 through 14. Two other groups of children, one of eighth graders (about 13 years old) and the other of tenth graders (about 15 years old), were interviewed only one time using similar questions. The study found that in children certain concepts developed significantly during childhood: pragmatic concerns, stereotypes of good and bad persons, role taking (acquiring the perspective of the other person), and positive affect relating to consequences. However, other concepts developed more slowly, with the sign * denoting especially *slow growth*: Improving the community or society*; responsibility to uphold laws, duty, norms; generalised reciprocity (exchange not on a one to one basis, but of benefit to a larger group); sympathetic concern for others*; negative affect relating to consequences; positive or negative* affect regarding living up to internalised values; protecting individual rights; preventing injustices to others*; equality of individuals*. The study also found that the oldest children were the most motivated by physical, material, or psychological needs of the other person, but were also the most likely to have stereotyped views and pragmatic concerns. Moreover, although reasoning generally increases with age, some intellectual areas actually *declined* in most children from ages 13-16.

This study presents a troubling picture of modern society, when people are at a stage in life when they have responsibility and power, but do not have the inclination to use these resources wisely. It also implies that young people have no larger concept of life, no vision of themselves or the future. The authors of the above study are strangely quiet about this finding, with the only substantive comment being that 'categories of reasoning were used quite infrequently'.[1] Even though the researchers were specifically concerned with trends of moral reasoning during childhood, they could hardly have overlooked the larger social relevance of their findings.

As moral comprehension is considered essential to the formation of proper relationship ideals, it is disturbing that a 15-year-old individual, whose reasoning abilities are really no better than a five-year-old's, might become entangled with high-stakes physical and emotional intimacies. Processes of integrity such as sympathetic reasoning, conscience relating to violation of own norms, an ambition to see equality, justice, in a better world, are hardly developed, yet these are necessary in establishing a solid, lasting intimate friendship.

There is little question that 'other-oriented concerns and per-spective-taking tendencies are intimately involved in moral reason-ing'.[2] Such concerns and tendencies are fostered by parents, rela-tives, and other adults, who must give children a wide-ranging understanding of human behaviour, and clearly defined behav-ioural boundaries. Further research finds that moral judgement of children throughout the teenage years is largely dependent on positive intra-family *relationships* and stimulation of moral reason-ing, more than on family *structure*.[3] Teenage children of authorita-tive parents use the most moral or post-conventional reasoning, followed by children of permissive parents, then authoritarian parents.[4] Note that *authoritative* in this context means parental status that is obtained through the gaining of respect, as opposed to *authoritarian*, where parental status is obtained through fear and force.

Thus, if a child lives in a family matrix of positive, beneficial relationships, then there is a very good chance the child will de-velop mature reasoning abilities, and consequently, act in a morally appropriate manner in all situations. However, if a young person cannot evaluate the moral components of a situation, due to poor upbringing, he will not be able to judge accurately the benefits and costs of an action. In other words, he cannot determine who has gained, who has lost, who made the right choice and who made the wrong choice in any given situation. This inability will un-doubtedly lead him to commit errors in social transactions, since in his estimation, one action will not be clearly provide better results than another action.

We earlier said that it is difficult to remove subjectivity from decision-making, and those young people who have trouble weighing all the factors of real life will raise a screen shutting out the consequences of the real world. Indeed, young people who actually go on to commit inappropriate behaviour not only admit they have little concern about morals, or about hurting other people's feelings, but moreover, they tend to confuse fiction with real life.[5] Life in these instances is seen as a 'movie', with events turning out the way the audience wants. This is not to say that social influences, such as from culture, media or education, are always negative. These factors might make a major positive impact on the development of moral reasoning, especially ones that encourage democratic processes, active decision-making, and mutual responsibility.[6] However, if a child is already predisposed to having a self-centred and autonomous mentality, then irresponsible social actions, including reckless sexual activity, will not be considered a fault, weakness, defect, or mistake. Film and television enterprises, due to structural limitations and marketing strategies, rarely address moral consequences in their productions, and many things simply 'happen' in a story, with little examination of causes or consequences. People 'fall in love', a girl 'has a baby', a man 'cheats on his wife'—these are merely plot developments, rarely accompanied by scenes showing serious ramifications, penalties, or costs.

Indeed, a natural outgrowth from undeveloped reasoning mechanisms is the inability to properly *assign responsibility* for inappropriate behaviour. Judgement of 'fault' is based not on sound principles, but on subjective aspects such as appearance, status, or likability. A study investigated more closely these dynamics. A sample of 8th graders from the Northwest United States were given hypothetical scenarios. In one case, a teacher angrily reprimands a student who disrupted the class by loudly asking someone else for lunch money. The moral implications of the incident are simple to understand: The teacher was wrong for reacting irritably, and the student was wrong for speaking in class. Despite the apparent clarity in such situations, assigning culpability is still a difficult task for many Americans; on the survey, many students demonstrated confusion, or clearly showed a tendency towards anti-sociability. In fact, 26% of the males got none, or only one answer right, out of a total of four such questions.[7]

There are negative sequellae that emerge from poorly developed reasoning faculties, as inability to objectively assess correctness will lead to protective measures that further impair interaction. This is especially true in the case where an person feels he is being unfairly treated, and will use deception as a countermeasure. For instance, if speaking in class is morally acceptable, then lying to say it did not happen is also acceptable, as a means of protecting oneself from unreasonable exercise of authority. Where one's personal agenda is at stake, such as passing a test necessary for success in career, mendacity is most likely to occur.[8] Dating relationships are likely contexts for dishonesty to manifest itself, because young men, in order to bolster their feeling of self-worth, want to create a 'match' as quickly as possible. Such weakness takes the form of falsely claiming that one is in love, or asserting that one wants to continue the relationship when one does not, or making statements that appear to predicate the relationship on sexual intimacy.[9]

The overall situation seems clear. Children naturally desire support through friendship with others, graduating from a state of reliance to one of alliance, a process of increasing closeness—first with family members, then with friends, and then with the opposite sex. Although this process of refining the concept of companionship is natural, the development of mental faculties that put into practise this concept are not. Such faculties must be conscientiously improved by the child's guardians in a clear, sustained effort. Due to the failings of parents and community, young persons often lack the comprehension of moral principles that produce profitable relationships. They sense that they cannot acquire 'love' from their family, so they press a partner 'into service' in order to gain the absent advice and support. It is easy to see how conflicts in dating relationships can multiply, as both persons make false charge and countercharge, a situation which is exacerbated by the increasing variety and depth of deception practised by young men and women.

Thus, in the modern age, young people take on adult responsibilities too early in their mental development, and engage in possessiveness, manipulation, and physicality, instigating difficult male-female relationship experiences. The individual has great difficulty cultivating a standard response, wherein he takes into account the necessity to strictly follow sensible rules, and wherein he is concerned with the well-being of others, especially those who are not directly affected by his behaviour. Lying becomes an easy way out of difficult situations, facilitated by his lack of interest in his behaviour's negative effects. Egotism, fantasy proneness, escapism, and prejudice figure prominently in the decisions that lead to how individuals deport themselves; goading themselves into habitual use of inspection, accumulation of evidence, categorisation, and careful evaluation is evidently beyond their willpower.

In short, *a deterioration of social interaction has occurred due to poor use of reasoning mechanisms*. Undoubtedly, fulfilment of self-centred, materialistic wants are obtained through crude generalisations, and lying, cheating, evasion, are necessary to avoid failure and discovery of deviance. However, what is even worse than the poor social interaction that is engendered by an inability to logically perceive moral principles, it is a degradation of ideals that will undermine all relationships. The hallmark of the person who possesses weak evaluative mechanisms is an inadequate response to the complexities of intimate male-female relationships. Such people do not have the courage to believe in themselves, and to stand up for the correctness of their actions. Consequently, it is inevitable that will fail to produce a healthy vision of intimate relationships and family life.

What we have said about the development of the various components of human desire, need, and ability can be subsumed under the term *individuation*. During life, a person grows from being a child, largely interchangeable with other children, to a fully formed adult, with his own identifiable traits. Nonetheless, what makes a person distinctive is not simply a collection of prosaic observations, but the belief that he can achieve the exemplary. This type of person possesses ideals, and the tools to bring them to life, which gives him an authentic 'uniqueness', an *individuality*. In this scenario, a person's collection of beliefs, experiences, strengths, and weaknesses are not simply derived from membership in a group, ethnos, community, or culture, but come from a profound struggle to arrive at the whole truth. An historical analysis of European societies (Sporer 2010A) shows how communities could integrate, with effectiveness and sensitivity, the social aspects of courtship and marriage contracts, with the personal ideals of love and companionship. We see, by comparison, that the average or typical modern marital relationship is clearly defective.

To answer the question posed at the beginning of the chapter, in the modern age the changes in family life have adversely impacted the average person's ability to individuate, and limited his capacity to address the challenges of the intimate or companionate relationship with confidence and effectiveness. We therefore need to examine more closely how the modern person conceptualises the family, where he is weak in evaluation, and what people in his social environment are causing him to be weak. Moreover, it is pointless to recommend making changes in behaviour in order to improve a situation, if the people involved in that situation lack the ability, or the willpower, to properly assess all the parameters that are involved.

Thus, we must research and discuss the individual's mental activity that forms the image of family life, before the individual himself forms a family in real life. The concept of family is universal, but it develops in manifold ways, depending on a variety of personal and social factors. Accordingly, we are not so much investigating what is contained within the concept itself, but the mechanisms that form the concept.

In the chapters that follow, it will become apparent that our European ancestors had a superior standard of individual accomplishment, and there is much that we can learn from the people who lived in traditional times. We shall see how older European cultures believed it was important to teach children about mutualism and reciprocity from a young age, by elaborating on those aspects that strengthen and solidify a relationship. Family structure factors were significant, since positive mental qualities could only be gained in households where one-to-one relations provided meaningful information, advice, and training. In these families, children developed evaluative mechanisms early in life, allowing them to correctly ascertain appropriate behaviour. Further, parents encouraged their children to form their own rules and values, as preparation for the day when they would take their position in a complex and changing society. Perhaps most importantly, parents wanted their children to look at all facets of a situation, not only parts of it. Social principles are ineffective when applied piecemeal, and so children were encouraged to prioritise and bring together these ideas into an integrated whole by using mature, advanced methods.

The modern age lacks many of these characteristics, and so we should address certain questions: How does a person take the various ideas pertaining to family and put them together into a usable, viable enduring integrated concept? Do people give much consideration to these factors? Do they evaluate the situation with reason and forethought, or with bias and subjectivity? How important are maturity and reasoning power in these areas?

Impulsu et caeca magnaque cupidine ducti conjugium petimus.
We, led by the impulse of our minds and by blind passion, desire marriage.

    JUVENAL (AD 55-c 127)

For this cause shall a man leave his father and mother, and be joined unto his wife, and they shall be one flesh.

    EPHESIANS 5:31 (KJV)

Chapter 2

Sharing, Consideration, and Mutual Reliance

*C*ritical situations occur in the lives of young people which cause them distress, because their behaviour produces unanticipated consequences, such as punishment or loss of reward. If one is to receive appropriate recompense, then one must choose a course of action obtained from a socially acceptable set; in the case of interpersonal relations, a situation can be described as having a 'moral quality'. As children do not have the mental faculties to recognise morally appropriate patterns of behaviour, it is logical to expect them to rely upon the elucidating advice of adults, who have themselves undergone similar experiences, and can disclose the advantages or disadvantages of a particular behaviour in a particular situation. We can visualise this process of discovery as an inverted pyramid, where a young person first draws on his own limited experiences and immature thinking processes; being frustrated with the results gotten thereof, he then proceeds to ask his friends, who have some more knowledge than he does; he then asks his parents, who can rely on an even wider range of personal experiences and second-hand information; and being not entirely comfortable with this, he then moves to the upper reaches of this structure, where information is at its widest and most secure, because it distilled from the experiences of literally thousands, or millions, of people. This last resource is the 'collective acumen', the hard-won wisdom distilled from centuries of multifarious incidents and conflicts, and passed down through generations using cultural mechanisms. Although information about social interaction that is acquired first-hand from a parent's own experiences can be effective, a young person might have avail himself of deeper cultural knowledge. In societies undergoing major changes, even middle-aged adults might not be able to provide appropriate moral principles derived from personal observations and participation. In such cases, a parent's greater experience in the matters of the world does not guarantee that they will have *acted correctly themselves*.

Basic needs never leave the individual, and so always remain part of the personality, but comprehending the dynamics of interpersonal relations is a necessary step in the process of individuation, as relationships, whether inside the family or outside, are the building blocks of social existence. Every individual enters adulthood full of expectations, but not necessarily full of knowledge. The intimate relationships is, of course, the apotheosis of friendship, and it is incumbent upon both persons, the members of the 'group of two', to take the necessary steps to create a workable arrangement. Hence, any temporary or short-term problems can be overcome, if the longer-term pattern of behaviour by both people has been visualised. These short-term obstacles are not large compared to the rewards that await in a future transformed by support and affection, sharing and positive mutual reliance. Steps must be taken in order to build up stability in finances and career. This long-term plan must be visualised before it can be accepted as viable. For example, a man dating a woman who attends law school must take into account the fact that when she graduates she will, for at least a few years, work very long hours. If he finds this unacceptable, then intimacy might diminish or end altogether.

Consequently, before all else, in the area of male-female relationships one must develop *preferences* as to what one finds desirable in a man or woman, to set *expectations* about married life, and to determine *priorities* so that these expectations can be met. These steps, however, must be carried out with objectivity.

It is clear that, for there to be genuine attraction between two people, there must be the perception that each person can *rely and trust the other, in all circumstances.* The underlying force of this perception comes from examining the opinions and attitudes of the other person, and determining that there is indeed *concordance.* How else will we know that a person will react in a certain way to a situation, in a manner congruent to our own interests, unless we 'sound out' their views? Therefore, tensions can only be resolved through *cooperation, consideration, and sacrifice*, without which the long-term viability of a relationship is impossible. For the sake of the relationship, every shrewd person appraises the present and future pragmatic and emotional characteristics of the other, in a sincere, thoughtful, and exhaustive study; considering the consequences, anything less would be reckless.

However, these pro-social concepts should not be misconstrued. No matter how much a person wants to demonstrate their love for another person, both people must first establish themselves as mature social 'entities', reasonably confident and independent. Thus, in traditional times, it was not selfishness or materialism that motivated the individual to wait for the time when his household would be secure and relatively free from financial worries, but rather, it was his deep concern for his future family's welfare.

Although it is true that many couples in the past might have been able to eke out a living before achieving economic solidity, such as through inheriting property, the dangers of such a situation were many. A loving relationship might have been attained, but within a precarious context. A man might have thought, What sort of husband would I be if I let my wife and my children starve? The concern for material security might be for oneself, or it might be for oneself *and* others. We can see that a critical part of the individuation process is to develop a self-assured and responsible nature in relation to the material things in life, by living out, or *reifying*, the virtues of empathy and caution. It is a dangerous assumption that strict adherence to financial protocols is a negative quality, only limited to simple-minded and cold-blooded egotists. The present cynical age has many critics who contend that the driving ambition in life is not love, but to reach a high material standard, with a concomitant predilection for autonomy and separation from others. When one steadfastly accumulates money and property before marriage, it is, they argue, only to protect one's own physical welfare, and a spouse and children are added merely as part of a further effort to fulfill that end. But it should be evident to anyone who takes the time to carefully observe human nature, that it is a considerate, sharing, and kind nature that impels a man or woman to gather together the appropriate and necessary funds in anticipation of marriage.

One must probe the 'health' of attraction, which constitutes the beginning of personal independence, and thus forms the foundation for later developments. Because of what he or she might substantively bring to a relationship, there are a wide variety of ways that the individual can be made attractive to another person. When drawing up the list of 'attributes of the opposite sex', does one appreciate or favour these attributes because social forces instruct that this is what it is to be, in the gender sense, a 'man' or 'woman', disregarding the personal implications? There is a cultural archetype of 'every-man's dream woman' and 'every-woman's dream man' which includes a whole set of characteristics. People should ask themselves whether their attraction is *genuine and authentic*, or whether it exists because society essentially handed them a 'list' that tells them what makes for a 'good' man or woman. Hence, what is considered attractive might be tainted by modern materialistic notions. In the modern context, the concept of the 'ideal' has devolved into a mere 'notion', where the sought-after situation is not truly the apotheosis, but a fantasy construct that does not take into account the realities. It is difficult for many to truly believe that they are becoming intimate with a real man or woman on the other side, not just a projection or image.

Attractiveness, although always appealing to the emotions, can nevertheless be a dangerous trap, as men and women are often blind to the actual components of the other's personality. Is the affable, caring, devoted woman a man sees really there, or is it just an illusion? Is the strong, decisive, protective man a true assessment, or is it merely a deception? A positive attribute is often perceived as being 'cloaked' by a negative trait, or there are contradictory traits that are both considered 'positive'. For example, a person should be sensitive but also forceful; accessible but protective; candid but gentle; cooperative but unyielding, thoughtful but confident. Since culture and genetics do much to differentiate the sexes, the individual must be careful to assess whether what they feel is simply attributable to a pre-existing concept of 'acceptability', or whether they truly feel drawn by the positive features of the other person.

People often find it intolerable that anything should deviate from their personal plans, so they mentally project what they wish to see on a situation, person, or object. The financial markets, for example, would behave in a distinctly unprecedented fashion if everyone based their investment decisions on carefully obtained objective truth, and avoided avaricious, quick-money schemes that bias judgement. Likewise, the unpredictable relations between men and women would become more stable if personalities were assessed using objective criteria.

Society can easily link personality attributes to physical attributes, precisely because the latter are so much clearer than the former. In many cultures, physical traits frequently have corresponding personality traits, which might or might not be accurate. For example, a tall, muscular man will be 'virile' and 'decisive', a small, curvaceous women will be 'undefended' and 'adaptable'. A prominent physical trait can often mislead people into thinking that the individual has control or mastery over an intellectual or emotional factor often associated with that trait. Hence, in parts of the world where the sexes are more dimorphic, that is, where the average man and woman are noticeably different from each other in many physical traits, evaluation is possibly more problematic. Do a 'he-man' and a 'baby-doll' fall in love because they erroneously believe each has a command over his or her own gender-specific psychological traits, basing their opinion only on a casual inference from their physical features?

Being fully aware that the differences one sees might not be universal but dependent on culture or genetics, accidents of time and place, makes one think twice before becoming seriously involved. Knowledge of standards and norms is the best antidote for self-deception, and the quickest road to maturity. But imagination also has a role, and must be utilised effectively. Putting ourselves mentally in other scenarios, where things might function equally well, or better, makes us question our assumptions about what is 'good' in a present situation. Short-term thinking must eventually give way to longer-term perspectives. The attraction between the sexes is ongoing because it is a way for the individual to bring more pleasure into his life, as one is often inclined to improve or upgrade one's personal situation.

Nonetheless, there are universal principles that are apparent to all people. One person must have more than just detailed knowledge about another person in order to make their relationship 'intimate', both have to understand each other's position, they must see life together in a truly 'conjoint' way. Mutuality is a way of gaining strength, through the joining of two people together who share a vision of their lives. For this to occur, however, the other person must be sensitive and considerate, and they must be able to put aside their own perspective at times to see the other viewpoint. Accordingly, the 'goodness' that a person feels about someone else invariably has to do with how much one person can *empathise* with another. Relationships are, in one way or another, always affected by the *congruity of ideas* that pass between people.

Even if a principle is universally comprehended, it does not mean that everyone will incorporate this principle into routine existence with the same effectiveness. This issue can be seen in the difficulty of correctly differentiating between the 'empathy' and 'sympathy'. Sympathy can be defined as an affinity, association, or relationship between persons wherein whatever affects one similarly affects the other. Empathy can be defined as the action of understanding, being aware of, being sensitive to, and vicariously experiencing the feelings, thoughts, and experience of another, of either the past or present without having the feelings, thoughts, and experience fully communicated in an objectively explicit manner. Sympathy is a simple 'resonance' between two people, who are connected in an ongoing situation, the details of which must be obvious. The emotional reaction to a situation that one person experiences will evoke a similar, although not necessarily equal, reaction in the other person. Empathy requires greater maturity, awareness, and mental facility. It requires greater imagination, an ability to see things from another person's perspective in an abstract manner. Nevertheless, empathy does not require an emotional reaction, only understanding. As a result, it is not enough only to sympathise with another person, because the bond that would exist is limited to what is visible; the thoughts, aims, intuitions, etc. of the other person would not be taken into account. Empathy is a more powerful force, as it creates a union which is deeper and consequently more permanent.

The trait of empathy has also developed slowly with young people. The multifarious challenges of modern living make adolescents crave confirmation of their own ideas; this unprecedented *strong desire for validation* is exercised in many social situations, utilising all accessible people of significant standing. In this regard, such persons quickly establish a 'mutual admiration society', where one person supports and validates the ideas of another. For this dynamic to be sustained, there must be fundamental similarity between the various participants.

The importance of similarity between partners is quickly understood as being predicated on a desire for immediate affinity, open friendliness, and an easy-going closeness. This quick formation might give them both the impression that they are living up to their moral values, of being 'pro-social'. There is no doubt that it is considered a positive trait to possess a belief in the equal status of men and women, but equality in social standing between the sexes does not mean that men and women have approximately the same attitudes, views, experiences, and beliefs. We are by nature attracted to a clearly defined entity called the opposite sex, but what about the 'opposite gender' whose attributes are not so obvious? Further examination must be carried out, in order to comprehend the full range of attributes.

It is self-evident, that the most positive use of diversity is for compensation of one's own weaknesses or inexperience, in which case similarity still plays the main role in the relationship, with dissimilarity also playing a supportive role. In this way, power can be attained through affiliation and compensatory validation. But support, by definition, means gaining from someone else something that one lacks. It also implies a certain deficiency, since to rely on another means losing power and autonomy. It is a reflexive response in human nature to praise independence, since one cannot be respected for one's accomplishments, if they are largely the result of other people's actions.

Yet, defective relationships are common, because great social pressure, coupled with immaturity, yields a strong desire for emotional sustenance. Once this desire is set into motion as a strategy, the individual is making an unintentional symbolic admission that there is a certain weakness in his character. Thus, modern concepts of dating and relationships are ambiguous to say the least, where they put great emphasis on *dependence*, but tempered with at least a few major reservations. The concept of family has been modified so as to make the individual more desirous than ever to experience love (support, desirability, praise) early and frequently, with the *quality* of that love being made secondary.

There is no disgrace or shame in wishing to reach one's goals through the assistance of another, as long as there is no dishonesty and no misuse of favours, and as long as one will also help the other person reach their goals with the same care one works to satisfy one's own aims. Indeed, one sign of maturity is the belief in reciprocity, where a person helps another and rationally expects assistance in return. However, reciprocity can also be viewed as one person contributing to the welfare of society, without expecting direct, immediate compensation. Yet, in a materialist culture, where physical gratification takes precedence over that of emotional satisfaction, it is difficult to extend one's perceptional latitude to include anything beyond the present situation. There is often a fine line between exploitation and acceptable employment of resources, between manipulation and making the best use of what one has. Further, many persons fear that they will be exploited in a relationship precisely because they are prone to certain lapses in judgement and 'frailty' in their interpretative processes.

Dissimilarity implies that sacrifice has to be made and there must be recompense. There is also the question of whether to proceed to next level of mutuality, since, although similarity can be viewed from positive moral perspectives, involving community and justice, dissimilarity seems to carry with it only hazards. If one is not inclined to sacrifice part of one's 'territory' in order to please a partner with different views and beliefs, then the relationship assumes a contingent character, where each step forward requires the fulfilment of certain criteria.

In a relationship involving two people of diverse personalities, since one is acknowledging a sacrifice of personal choice, when one depends on a steady dating partner for emotional satisfaction, the relationship must offer a *repayment for that sacrifice* in some substantial way. The traditional view is that this usually entails a transformation of lifestyle, from being alone (dissipation and deficiency) to living together (concentration and synergy), either with or without marriage. *To not proceed* to the next level of marriage would be, in the view of those who believe in this concept, foolish as one would lose one's investment, in the same way as working in a job that does not make use of one's college education, or building up a career for several years in one occupation, only to begin at the bottom of the ladder in another.

Open and frequent dialogue about these matters of mutuality would come about, yet even informal discussions about the subject are rare, especially when the attraction is based largely on similarities. Perhaps this is due in part to the fact that from a public policy perspective, which deals with short-term issues that have direct social impact, little can be said about the phenomenon of seeking similarity. One hardly ever hears that a similarity in opinion between two people is responsible for provoking a fight. Social authorities have more to say about diversity, since this can initiate divisions not only within a household, but in other areas of society. Consequently, issues related to the building of constructive intimate relationships that are discussed publicly often have poor scope and depth. A general belief in the similarity of the sexes might be in line with the demands of modern society. As discussed in Sporer (2010C), modern culture tends to praise similarity and downgrade dissimilarity, because society demands more flexibility to take on the tasks of a changing industrial economy, with the result being less commitment and less willingness to change.

Every person must ascertain what level of similarity and difference he prefers in the opposite sex, even if external forces attempt to make the decision for him. An individual's personal set of ideals, developed early on in life, balances a mix of similarity and diversity of basic ideas and opinions. As a result, everyone has the basic capacity to deal with interpersonal differences. The individual must seek out the truth for himself, when family and society fail to provide appropriate guidance, and he must visualise how a relationship can fill in those gaps in knowledge and abilities that are precisely due to the limitations of social institutions. However, although congruence in traits is easily determined, the level of dissimilarity is not, and making a good match between personalities is difficult. If certain differences produce a justified fear, then the divergence in personality can become the basis for an end to the relationship. Some might see differences as a type of injustice due to the feeling that there is inequity, that one holds a better position or higher rank than the other. Both might work equally hard in maintaining the relationship, but one appears to benefit more.

Incongruously, the allure of diversity proves strong, yet young people hardly ever understand the potential good that can come from two people utilising each other's individualised knowledge, experiences, and perspectives within a lifelong association. The differences that people see in each other might be intriguing, but simple allure does not produce genuine fulfilment; the benefits of cooperative association can only be realised in the *long-term*, in circumstances where the two are closely working together. Thus, what people initially desire from a relationship is mutual support, but what eventually pulls them in more deeply could very well be a set of interlocking positive *differences*.

The thinking of our European ancestors is difficult to interpolate into the container of modern culture, tightly packed as it is with notions, musings, caprices, half-grown ideas, underripe assertions, puerile musings, falsehoods and fantasies. Traditional concepts were poetic: Each person in the relationship has made significant allowances in his or her mind and heart to accommodate the other; each has sculpted from the days a contour that cannot be filled by anyone else but that special person, a 'favourite'. Therefore, it was expected that both dependence and independence to some extent be experienced *simultaneously*.

We can see that young people are burdened with the demands of maintaining independence in peer groups, education, and career. They use intimacy as a *substitute* for affection and as a way to deepen the relationship, and they also make poor decisions in dealing with a dating partner because of their immaturity. We can see that self-serving interests are often at the heart of evaluations between men and women. Behind these limitations, there is a clear dearth of moral reasoning, and it appears that positive social values are learned with difficulty, and important principles are ignored. When the individual has an immature personality, weak mental processes, and a love ideal that is in constant struggle with materialism and social status, then the major goal must be that of finding similarity over that of differences.

Hence, in the modern context, the concept of family life tends to be based on a parsimonious model that takes relatively few factors of personality, background, and experiences into account. Further, a spirit of independence often arouses in people a desire for similarity in relationships, for it is these factors that are instrumental in realising one's goals and finding a good life—a life that incorporates security and stability, as well as progressivity. Because of the simple-minded use of another person as a crutch, the character of the intimate relationship itself is prone to denigration as a result, because it is not being used for its ultimate purpose, that of establishing an environment where mutuality is the main dynamic.

Consequently, in the realm of the intimate relationship, security appears to be more important than finding happiness. We note that teenage friendships are controlled largely by one important dynamic we have been discussing: The peer relationship provides a path for happiness, but only when it stresses reinforcement of personal ideas as a means of emotional support. This concept of a 'family' is clearly poorly conceived, yet social stresses make it difficult to fully work out a mature ideal. We shall now investigate see how people plan for the future, and whether they take into account the full range of features that married life has to offer, and how the search for compatiblity affects the age of dating, and closeness, and seriousness of marriage; future aim, plan, continue, next step, dating age, communications, compatible, temporary,

Let us now explore more closely how these issues of security, empathy, attraction, and moral values operate in the lives of young people, in their pursuit of establishing a viable relationship.

To live with someone and to live in someone are two fundamentally different matters. There are people in whom one can live without living with them, and vice versa. To combine both requires the purest degree of love and friendship.

JOHANN WOLFGANG VON GOETHE (1749-1862)

He was reputed one of the wise men that made answer to the question, when a man should marry?
'A young man not yet; an elder man not at all'.

FRANCIS BACON (1561-1626)

Chapter 3

Marriage as a Natural Outcome

*I*nteraction between the sexes has, of course, always been regulated to some extent, the rules being based on the concept of individual maturity. In European cultures, it was commonly assumed that the interaction of the sexes would continue for some years down a 'path' of growing intimacy, with marriage the final, natural outcome. The morally 'correct' ages at which the path began and ended were usually a function of various economic, educational, cultural, and religious components. In the early 20th century, maturation was viewed as a gradual process, which culminated by about the age of 21, after which boys and girls no longer 'matured' in the sense of needing to learn about fundamentals, but rather started to put into practise the knowledge they had gained. There were, however, markers of maturity before that age. For example, the 'sweet-16' party or the debutante's ball was the 'coming-out' ritual where the girl became a woman, at least physically, and thus began the long road of experiencing adult activities. Nonetheless, physical and mental maturity are not perfectly correlated, and it was thought that young people still need several years after physical maturity to reach a minimal level of psychological competence. Consequently, considering the responsibilities of married life, marriage could 'decently' take place only after 21.

Despite these general views, society not only approved, but encouraged interaction between young boys and girls, as long as they were supervised. Indeed, by mid-century the age at which boys and girls began to participate in joint activities was as low as 12. It was thought that such interaction would build character in both sexes, thus removing the fears or self-consciousness that might interfere with later dating. The lowering of the age of supervised interaction between the sexes not surprisingly led to concomitant declines in age in unsupervised interactions. In the years following the Second World War, the age at which individuals began to date was about 16, and has been declining since that period.

Although there might be general rules that govern the interaction between boys and girls, and young men and young women, there are more specific considerations that are unique to each type of relationship that is formed. Indeed, in the case of dating or courtship type relationships, we can identify three substantive factors found in Western societies that effectively regulate socialising patterns.

First, there is the difficulty in determining where a prospective love interest is currently in an intimate relationship. This is especially true in the case of discovering the availability status of girls. Enquiries about a girl's status might be made through the 'grapevine', although this information is often unreliable. More likely, boys must steel themselves to go through the sometimes embarrassing ordeal of asking out a girl for a date, in order to find out whether she is available. Of course, if she turns the boy down, she might be available, but simply does not care to associate with that particular boy.

Second, boys do not like to be turned down for dates. Dating is a test of their attractiveness at a time when they are very vulnerable as to identity and self-worth; the more failures, the greater the blow to their manhood, even if the refusals to go out on dates are because the girl is already dating someone else.

Third, young people, in the conventional thinking of modern society, must always have a boyfriend or girlfriend, but *longevity* is not a requirement. In this regard, a girl may date someone for a few months, then break this off, and then quickly gain another boyfriend, whom she sees for another few months before breaking off with him. This type of pattern in cultures that do not tolerate more than one close male friend per girl at one time clearly makes it difficult for boys to 'cut in', and get the chance to become friendly with her. Moreover, many other girls have fairly lengthy relationships, where there are few breaks in the relationship chain, again making it difficult for boys to find unattached girls. For example, a teenage girl with school and other obligations tries to keep a boyfriend as well in her 'schedule', in order to adhere to a strategy. Her other activities might bring her satisfaction, but the stress arising directly and indirectly from those activities makes her feel inadequate without a boyfriend, especially if close female friends each have one.

To an extent, the implementation of these three factors within a particular social environment affects the participants' concept of family life, since they point to sex-related characteristics that will potentially affect the marital situation, long after the dating phase has ended. Consequently, if boys and girls have pleasant meetings, arranged cooperatively and without much difficulty, then their view of each other, both as individuals and as members of a sex, will likely be positive. Further, their view of family life will also be positive, since they will believe that the role of spouse is to secure happiness and tranquillity within the household. However, if the dating experiences are negative, laced with frustration, recriminations, and embarrassment, then the concept of family life will probably be altered so as avoid reliving these painful feelings. These factors can legitimately be called 'modern', for they did not all exist in the traditional era, although certain aspects might be universal.

As long as young people can maintain close supportive contact with parents and other adult relatives, then their need for such relationships with others, such as with peers, would be minimal. Interestingly, the decreasing attention given by parents to their children's development in pro-social thinking and moral reasoning has caused young people to explore social areas outside of the household, in order to find experiences of a truly meaningful character. Hence, a single formidable issue emerges in the modern context: Young people do not receive enough parental attention at home and seek affection and support elsewhere. The widespread domestic disruption in contemporary society leaves young people feeling unloved and alone. Forging ties with aunts, uncles, grandparents, and cousins might be attempted, but they find them either unwilling or preoccupied by their own domestic problems. Turning to people their own age for solace is the easiest solution to this problem, not to create a relationship built on mutual respect, but one precariously constructed on rudimentary affinity. Although in many cases the *present* need for love might not be overwhelming, predicted *future* needs are being taken into account. However, these early relationships develop in a way that is not compatible with the concept of intimacy, and so are not authentic or genuine. This has a major impact on the individuation process, and, consequently, affects the ability to handle the exigencies and challenges of life in a mature, confident, and effective manner.

We can see that the age at which these cross-sex interactions occur is important, since if they take place at lower ages, where the participants are of lower maturity, then there will undoubtedly be occurrences which taint expectations of happiness in the future family. The high demand for supportive partners pushes them into forming relationships at a lower age, although these associations cannot rightly be called 'companionate'. Therefore, young people seek supportive relationships, although not of the companionate variety, and this has forced certain restrictions on the formation of peer associations. In and of themselves the three factors discussed above do not necessarily lead to early dating experiences. However, when young people desire supportive relationships from opposite sex peers, then these factors serve to facilitate a lower dating age.

Since the early part of the 20th century, girls from a young age have had frequent and steady contact with members of the opposite sex; initiation of serious dating or 'courtship' began at about 18, an age close enough to the 'magical number' of 21 to be acceptable to society. Unfortunately, those boys who turned 18 found many girls to have already been taken by other boys, and so they were *excluded* from having a dating partner their own age. Since most adolescent boys, focussing on a ready-made similarities based on age, considered only girls from their own age group and two or three years below, and since younger age groups had not yet begun to date, there would logically be more potential partners if they sought girls *younger* then themselves. Thus, these boys, and younger siblings who had also noticed that they would have some difficulty dating at 18, began to date girls who were 17 or 16. Boys who were 17 anticipated the struggle to date at 18, and so began to search for girlfriends age 17 and 16, lest they be shut out.

When dating at a younger age became the norm for both sexes, finding unattached girls again proves difficult, and so boys move to the next lower age group of 16 and 15. This 'ratcheting down' effect continued to lower the age of dating. Even if a boy did not really desire a girlfriend at 13 or 14, he felt he had to obtain one if he were not to be left with no choices at an older age, when he foresaw the possibility that he would *very much* desire one. The only tangible lower limit on this pattern, which we might call an 'exclusion phenomenon', would probably be the onset of puberty.

We note that the decline in age of unsupervised dating is not due to a substantive change in social mores. Instead, it is the result of demographic factors activated by the desire in young people for immediate rapport with a boyfriend or girlfriend, through the finding someone of similar temperament, opinions, and knowledge. The three factors we mentioned earlier still operate, and they have facilitated the progressively lower age of social interaction between the sexes, within the confines of Western social structure.

Although dating has commenced at younger ages, this does not mean that young people are finding fulfilment in their desire for affiliation. What stands in the way is also age-related: The lower the age, the greater the divergence in views and attitudes between boys and girls. Hence, there is less *compatibility* between boys and girls at lower ages compared to later ages, and it is likely that there will be more conflict between boys and girls at younger ages. This might explain the fact that, although the age of dating has declined, the age of marriage did not come down as well. If people start to date at later ages, they will find more compatibility, since the process of age can often function in a way comparable to the process of education in changing opinions (see Sporer 2010C). One would expect that couples who inaugurate dating at an earlier age, say by the age of 15, would be similar to lower educated adults, as their education is the same as that of an adult but who finished school before completing secondary level requirements. Although formed at an early age, opinions go through a steady evolution throughout life, mediated by both the educational system and the intellectualisation process. Thus, younger teenagers would probably be more likely to *disagree* on various topics, such as whether they themselves should marry, whether marriage would affect their relationships with friends and relatives, and whether they should marry someone of a different race. Of especial importance is the divergence of views on whether good looks are a critical component in attraction, since teenagers put far more emphasis on these matters than do adults. In addition to a lack of maturity, an inability to concur on basic issues concerning life attitudes would make it quite difficult for young people to make close, intimate friendships.

Even with problems of compatibility, the youth of our day find that 'going steady' has an important place in their social life. We have seen that the quasi-family bond that young people form is motivated by a desire to find compensation for love and support lacking at home. Nonetheless, the lack of stability and durability of this relationship is the result of an external factor, that of the independence 'ethos', which prevents the relationship from taking a natural course. The inadequacy of moral reasoning in young men and women creates difficulties in undertaking appropriate roles in their intimate associations. But such inadequacy often results in a lack of forceful thinking, a hindrance to bold action; those who cannot 'figure out' the correct course of action will not be able to withstand social pressures. The modern lifestyle makes many demands on people, including being independent of ties, and one must have a good reason to deviate from this demand; if they do not, then they succumb to these demands. Consequently, more involved youthful relationships usually do not progress to marriage, as one or both participants are 'called away' to meet the criteria of an independent 'lifestyle'. As Gordon & Miller (1984) point out, perhaps unsurprisingly, young people do *not* view a short term commitment, such as 'going steady', as a prelude to marriage. Further, those who do go steady are *not* different from those who do not in terms of their level of opposite-sex socialising. This would indicate that young people see this kind of conviviality, of regular dating often accompanied by some kind of sexual activity, as a form of *pseudo*-marriage. They attempt to extract from a boyfriend or girlfriend the same kind of emotional satisfaction, advice, and warmth that they could obtain from a spouse. To this extent, dating can be used for many ulterior motives. Nonetheless, in certain cases, such relationships can be a form of *proto*-marriage, where once a pattern is set and the couple feel they are in love, they might push themselves to go beyond the *status quo*, to the next step of marriage.

However, as most young people are not prepared to make sacrifices, they use contrivances to create the illusion of a true bond. Almost inevitably, there is the descent into sexuality in order to make the relationship 'active', and to keep each person joined to the other. As the one-quarter proportion of girls who have had sexual experiences by 15 will attest,[10] more than a few communities harbour secluded intimate rendevous between boys and girls who are barely into puberty, without there being any serious consideration of marriage and all that it entails. In such a case, the mutually supporting relationship will have a tendency to fall apart, as the requirements made by peers, school, teachers, and others have to be fulfilled.[11] This confusion repeats itself over the course of early adulthood. In fact, in a study of five metropolitan areas, heterosexual males had on average eight partners, and females three partners by their mid-30s.[12] In another survey, for the age group of under 35, males had on average five sex partners, and females had three.[13]

Clearly, many young people cannot find a viable path to marriage which does not include sexual intimacy with 'steady' boyfriends or girlfriends. If they abstained from sexuality during this time, it would mean having to wait perhaps ten years or more between the beginning of the path (puberty), and the end of it (marriage). Moreover, social trends in the modern era have circulated the idea that a primary consideration of the male-female relationship was the fulfilment of a sexual 'need'. In spite of a reduction of casual sex since the 1970s, and a move toward 'committed partnerships', the belief in the necessity of relationship experimentation over the life course is still all too prevalent. Sexual activity as a major aspect of adulthood is a subject area in its own right. Yet, it is regrettable that one's 'beloved' is likely to be among numerous 'heartthrobs', 'crushes', 'sweethearts', 'affairs', and 'involvements', a lonely figure popping up at the end of a long line of failures.

We noted earlier (page 12), that, judging by the activities and standards of our time, young people lack a long-term vision of their own lives, and therefore, we can now say that they themselves, in reality, might not be sure whether an intimate relationship is a prelude to marriage, or merely a temporary contrivance. The plan for companionship has faltered. Among teenagers, who in recent times rarely look upon dating as being in any way a prelude to marriage, it is not uncommon to have many sex partners, and perhaps one or two 'true' loves.

This *conflict between emotional designs and pragmatic plans* has to constitute one of the more unreasonable aspects of modern social systems. The pattern might be repeated as follows: A girl of 17 or 18 finds herself strongly attracted to a boy who is around the same age. This strong affection is often 'fulfilled' by sexual activity. Now that this association has deepened, and the pair feel they are close 'partners', they might ask: Now what happens? Can we marry? Can we alter our lives for the sake of an early marriage? Almost all the time, the answer is a resounding 'No'. As the average age for marriage in more recent times is about 27 for both sexes, the current popular belief is that only country rubes or inner-city denizens would marry at such a young age. In keeping with the modern independence 'ethos', both young men and women probably expect to expend a great deal of mental and physical resources for college and career building, leaving little for a prospective spouse and children.

There is, furthermore, a disturbing trend in Western society to base relationships on amorphous and ambiguous 'feelings'. Long periods of separation, the temptations of alternative activities, the desire to experiment sexually, doubts about the existence of true affection—all imperil the youthful 'romantic' relationship. And without the feeling of 'romance', there can be no marriage in the modern age. The question which inescapably confronts people is similar to this: 'Is my boyfriend (girlfriend) only good for some conversation, having some fun, or is there something deeper here?' Unless, there is a true attraction, which, as we have shown, must be the result of competent, mature mental faculties, the relationship cannot continue, because whatever similarities and positive differences exist will never be utilised effectively.

We must understand, however, that ending a relationship is not easy. The couple have laboured so much to create a proper relationship, indeed a quasi-family bond, that it is genuinely difficult to break it off. Nonetheless, the weight of competing factors makes nearly all of these relationships ultimately bound for failure. Perplexity such as this can cause suspicion about the longevity of all male-female relationships, and suspicion can easily be conveyed to married life. A very negative message is therefore presented, in that *all* intimate relationships people have before their mid-20s are bound for failure. As a result, the ideal of independence is clearly being favoured in this context. What about those strong desires for fondness and affection? It is all for naught. The predominating dynamic is the pragmatic one, where 'affection' must be something one can turn on and off like a switch.[14]

We can see, though, that pushing young people into marriage is also unwise. Judging by the high divorce rates for young age groups, the avoidance of early marriage is justified. For Americans who married from age 18 up to the mid-20s, divorce rates are high, but there is a steady decline in divorce tendency over this range. However, the dissolution rate for couples who marry 'normally' at around age 25 still remains high.[15] This bears witness to the fact that many persons, even after finishing college and beginning a career, do not hold adequate proficiency to maintain their marriage in the putatively simpler environment of the family home.

Indeed, nowhere is the modern supremacy of the independence ethos more obvious, and the authenticity of married life more challenged, than in the phenomenon of relationship dissolution. For that reason, the divorce rate in a nation can be an important objective indicator of the weakness of the family concept. The higher the rate, the more important are fragmentary self-centred desires, and the less important are mature concepts of love. Whatever the specific causes, the sorrows of married people must be in some way an outgrowth of the modern concept of independence, with its tremendous urge for escape and solitariness carrying forward in residual form into adulthood.

The inability to stand up against the independence ethos leads to the majority of dating relationships ending, not with matrimony, but with an abrupt exit. The lack of appropriate mental development in both young men and women can be blamed, but it is these very weaknesses that also lead to unnecessary emotional harm. We have earlier discussed the problem of dishonesty in relationships (page 15), and noted that it is a form of protection from the consequences of poorly developed reasoning mechanisms. Moral reasoning, encompassing reciprocity, empathy, and consideration, are indeed lacking in the life of the average teenager, and 'depth' is, consequently, not a word in his vocabulary, much less a part of his romantic life. Besides the possible conflict in the relationship itself, even the circumstances of its termination can be incongruous with the goals of love and affection. Thus, the quick and easy route that leads out of the relationship is preferred.

Of those who gave a reason for a breakup, in about one in ten cases the individual will give a false reason as to why the relation-ship had to end (with women somewhat more likely to do this). The main reason for such deception is ostensibly to protect the feelings of the other person, but the real reason is usually a lack of continuing interest, or the fact that the person has found someone new.[16] Although falsehood might seem to be considerate if the real reason would cause distress, it can produce feelings of cynicism and animosity towards the opposite sex, since it undermines the whole process of communication. If honesty were universal, then perhaps dating and courtship would be less of an onerous and unpredictable experience. At the cost of hurt feelings, one would not be left to wonder what went wrong, or to remain helpless in self-deception.

Even when young people realise that they are incapable of han-dling these difficult matters, there is still a strong motivation to keep pressing a partner into intimacy. Hence, the emotional cost of the breakup of even a 'casual' relationship is often so profound that it can be a form of 'divorce', a situation greatly exacerbated by another common youth problem, that of substance abuse.[17] No doubt deceit, instability, forced intimacy, and the conflict between dependence and independence lead many to despondency. But there is more than this, for such emotional reactions are indicative that one or both persons were over-dependent. In fact, relationship issues can form a nexus of depersonalisation, contributing to de-pression and suicidalism. For those who have weakly developed personalities, the feelings of failure, deprivation, and rejection are intensified from the delay in resolving the conflict between inde-pendence and dependence. Thus, the various aspects emanating from the modern concept of independence—such as ulterior

motives, selfishness, recklessness, impermanence—become criti-
cally important components in the 'strategy' of social relations.
Such heedless decision-making underlines the high premium modern society puts on early dating, in spite of high costs associated
sexual activity, promiscuity, dissolution, conflict and depression.

The most straightforward solution, at present, to the problem of
unstable relationships that result from a poorly constructed and
unintegrated family concept, is to *increase the age* at which people
attempt to establish their first intimate association. The signs for
this are not encouraging, since, as we have seen, the age at which
people begin to date has become progressively lower throughout
this century. The dynamics in Western society that lead to lower
age of dating, means that young people will have even less power
to construct appropriate viable relationships, resulting in difficult
relations early in life, which in turn further distort ideals.

Increasing the length of courtship might also help, but in many
cultures, after dating for an extended period of time, the pressure
to marry also begins to build from friends and family, who often
do not take into account the couple's desire for a natural course of
events. Is there an objective measure of time over which this 'natural' course evolves? Although a precise number can never be gotten,
when considering such an important proposition, it would clearly
be prudent to wait for at least three years, a time which allows the
couple to see each other in different circumstances, conditions and
challenges. Paradoxically, although young people seem to feel very
comfortable with the current dating arrangement which easily
brushes away questions of marriage, when it comes to dating their
future *marriage* partner, the dating relationship actually speeds up.
For Americans, the time of dating before marriage (courtship in-

cluding an engagement period) is on the average about one year, with about one-third taking more than three years, and only 7% taking five or more years.[18] A man and woman who take only a year between meeting and marriage might have settled on the idea of marrying each other after only six months, although neither might feel comfortable with the idea. At a time when it is not unusual for a person to take six months or more to decide on the kind of car or house to purchase, it is strange that people would spend less time deciding on something that is far more important to their lives, and far more difficult, if not impossible, from which to free themselves. When moral values are not taught by parents and adequately assimilated by young people, then they are left to construct these ideas by themselves, with all the imperfections.

We can now see that the individuation process stalls when the desultory actions of young people make it difficult for them to reach a goal of establishing an enduring, fulfilling companionship. The family of childhood itself has become a major source of competing aims and contradictory values. It is clear that there is a necessity to assist the modern individual, who is often alone, confused, and struggling, with the competition between emotional, material, and social principles. Institutions stand to give the most efficient help, by providing instruction and answers to the most common questions through groups and mass market materials. When the individual is given the opportunity to interpret the similarities and differences that exist between himself and his prospective partner, there can only be an improvement in married life, but only as long as no other negative factors are introduced in the process. Many churches, for example, provide marital training or counselling before marriage as a way of smoothing the transition from single life to cohabitation. A typical course might meet, for example, on five consecutive Mondays, two hours each for a total of ten hours, with two hours homework, and three books to read. These courses cover, in varying levels of detail, the gamut of issues that pertain to married life: Finances, communication, sexual activity, and the rearing of children.[19]

Authority figures, especially when representing religious culture, often try to succeed where the parents have failed, and assist the young person in forming a more coherent model of marriage of family. The deficit in moral reasoning in the area of communications, in particular, can be remedied to an extent. Although one might think that the such means, such as courses offered by churches and other organisations, are admirable in preventing people from making rash decisions, and helping them prepare for the obligations of wedlock, there are a number of difficulties.

Firstly, by underscoring the issue of communications, means are made more important than substance. People might be forced to take on 'scripts' and to act in artificial ways which interfere with the individual's normal personality. Secondly, courses try to squeeze a large amount of information into a relatively short period of time, with the complexities of relationships, and thus their most important aspects, not getting enough attention. Thirdly, courses can cause embarrassment because they elicit personal and private information. A person in such a situation might think: Why should anyone, in a class or group designed for education, have to lay out their innermost thoughts and ideas to others for approval? Finally, these courses, by offering lessons in 'conflict-management' techniques, *anticipate* problems will occur between the couple. Whilst this might be realistic, should it not be paramount for a church to urge the individual to strive for perfection, to teach that it *is* possible to have a nearly problem-free marriage? It might be entirely appropriate that churches lead the way in helping people to understand each other. However, it is a contradiction to proclaim that God can make all things 'perfect', but then to imply that God cannot make the marital relationship 'perfect'; in such ways they damage their own credibility. By making concessions to 'inevitable' human weakness, the church's role as an authoritative institution that can give key insight into human nature is made untenable.

Moreover, while commendable in attempting to bring logic to the decision-making process, the use of tests and similar devices comes too late in the relationship. How are the couple to deal with the unenviable discovery that they are not compatible? As we have stated, the pressure to marry is already probably quite intense, because of their long-standing relationship. Now that they are engaged, the couple are under even more pressure to carry out the commitment they have made. Furthermore, tests give dubious ratings of normalcy; even researchers cannot agree, in most cases, what kind of pre-marital relationship will be converted into a successful marital one. The only exception to this, and it applies in only a minority of situations, is where the couple are openly and distinctly aberrant in their actions towards other people, or each other. On the whole, where experts do not concur on major points, examinations cannot be utilised effectively—and least effectively it seems in the busy but emotionally fragile weeks and months leading up to the wedding.

A superior solution to the problems of the poor reasoning faculties of youth would be if the various institutions of society would persuade individuals to get into the habit of generally *forming goals as a life-long pursuit.* Further, we would emphasise the building of *sound mechanisms,* and not the sale of standard and trite answers. Using instruments and courses in the effort to encourage people to form long- and short-term goals is a step in the right direction, but this makes no sense when the nuptials, only short weeks ahead, are fast approaching. By putting a couple into a position where they must 'find themselves', and make difficult decisions within this narrow time frame creates, not avoids, artificial and socially determined commitments. People should form their life goals and ideas about married life well before the wedding, and it is unwise to think they can form them almost on the spot.

Further, we should encourage young people to look beyond the current situation, by drawing from the well of traditional wisdom, which might give embolden them to envision how even the most ambitious status and career aims can successfully co-exist with love, affection, and commitment. If they studied European culture and history they would see that, as long as people are willing to share their lives in a true meaningful way with others, then status, companionship, and material security can all be achieved simultaneously. However, if the person will not use his intellect to guide his behaviour, other forces of an external origin will then do so.

Up there on the mountain,
there is a tall house,
And every morning
three fair maidens come out,
The first one is my sister . . .
the second is my friend . . .
The third has no name . . .
she must become mine.

DORT OBEN AUF DEM BERGE (German song, early 1500s),
LUDWIG SENFL (1486-1543)

Home life as we understand it is no more natural to us
than a cage is natural to a cockatoo.

GEORGE BERNARD SHAW (1856-1950)

Chapter 4

A Platform for Individuation

$\mathcal{S}$incere intentions are commendable, but in a social context of changing demographics, economy, and culture, as found in all industrialised nations, the mere intent to do what is good is rarely adequate. The people who have made the choice of founding their relationship without utilising traditional ideas are going to face dilemmas that can only be resolved by creating relevant moral principles through the objective interpretation of evidence. As we have seen, people have difficulty in recognising negative and inappropriate behaviour, and therefore they tend to structure their relationships in selfish ways. There is, in short, an inability to look outside of oneself.

Marriage is, necessarily, based on dedication and sacrifice, since familial harmony cannot occur without these things. However, another need, that of experiencing significant independent achievement, where the individual accomplishes major goals without major assistance, also demands satisfaction. From this arises a competition between two desires: The desire to secure commitment from a person of the opposite sex, and the desire to be free of making a personal commitment to that person. It is not an endorsement of selfishness to say that these desires are valid, but one cannot successfully find a way out of this dilemma by both obtaining commitment from someone else, and yet giving little of it in return, for such a relationship obviously cannot endure, and its termination will not be amicable. Clearly, two aims that could potentially take the individual in different directions cannot co-exist without forethought and planning.

Consequently, the process of individuation is fundamentally about balancing powerful, emotionally charged 'forces' that push or pull the individual. It might seem strange that, in order to create a viable concept of family, the individual must accommodate independence, since at first glance, family is about 'togetherness', but independence, and its corollaries such as autonomy, is about 'aloneness'. Nonetheless, upon closer examination, we cannot deny that the desire of independence is ubiquitous, and so *it must be somehow integrated into the concept of family*, as otherwise, the selfishness borne of undifferentiated independent tendencies could very well destroy the family life the individual is trying to build. In line with this reasoning, we need to examine more closely the various strands that form the concept of *independence*, in order to show what components of this concept can be successfully accepted into familial life.

Given the modern misinterpretations, conceptualising independence in all of its manifestations is a difficult task, but it is only after fully understanding the underlying strong emotional desire for intimacy and enduring companionship, *that we can understand what freedom really means to us*. The terms 'independence' and 'freedom' can be generally defined as a state of being where the individual's Will is not affected, controlled, or influenced by other people, things, groups, or institutions. However, these terms can be variously defined, and meaning is relative to the particulars of a situation. If two people are asked to imagine themselves in a certain situation, it is possible that one person might state he is in a 'free' condition, but the other person might not. And yet neither is incorrect, because as each person has his own unique set of goals, each one evaluates situational factors differently; the same attributes of a situation might be viewed as restraining by one, but irrelevant by the other.

Enjoying greater intimacy with others, such as with friends, acquaintances or a spouse, means there is less need for family, although one is still not a 'free man' or a 'free woman'. Once again, we must state that a person's external physical activity is not necessarily a true representation of inner mental activity. Current social standards might rate a person as 'free' because he has met certain general criteria, but that person himself might not believe he is 'free', no matter how many people tell him that he is.

Local or temporary examples of an escape from obligations are not proof of independence, since the individual might very well still be greatly dependent on other people. How many times do we see bohemian 'radicals' still depend on parents for money, friends for advice, government for protection, women for excitement, and drugs for enhancing or stabilising moods? Such 'libertines' have no individuality, because they possess no distinctive, functional, productive qualities. Simply demonstrating to others that one can do things that the average 'unfree' individual cannot do is not a sign of true liberty. Conversely, a butler might have his duties laid out for him in minute detail, and so he might appear quite dependent and without liberty, but because he is doing precisely what he wishes to do, offering important assistance to others *in his own individual manner*, he is genuinely independent. If he is drawing upon his personal skills, experience, knowledge, and talents, in order to reach an important goal, then the time and effort he gives over to someone else is simply an expenditure of resources *in pursuit of a goal*, it is a sacrifice that which will be repaid.

The desire for autonomy, when aligned with a mature, logical mind, is a sign of a healthy spirit seeking fulfilment in a world full of potential. Yet, we must be careful not to be swayed by popular prejudice that only focuses on the external: *Evidence of independence is not evidence of individuation*. An 'independent' person might attain his position through luck, contrivance, or coercion, but this is no true 'individual'. The person who is clearly on the path of individuation, who is cognisant of the importance of developing the Self, will use an intellectually driven schema to provide an effective realisation of personal goals. People must concentrate on doing whatever possible to individuate, to become truly free, which always means periods of sacrifice, change and learning. In other words, *to gain liberty, and to reach the ultimate goal of fulfilment, one must willingly be a servant of some kind*. Obviously, some independence must be given up in order to attain maximum contentment; thus, it is incumbent upon us to determine what we really need from life to be fulfilled. Each one of us must determine what encroachment on our freedom is acceptable, and what is unacceptable. Some compromise their goals in order to compensate for the buffeting crosswinds on the way to autonomy. Such a person might blame outsiders for denying him the ideal love, but by attaining the other ideal, that of independence, it is clear that he has only himself to blame for his predicament. No one can be both, *in toto*, free and unfree at the same time.

By visualising the process of moving increasingly outward—from individual to family to community to larger society—we can obtain more insight into the critical role that family has in promoting personal growth, and we will find a resolution to any conflicts between ideas. We therefore focus on the *individuation process*, where a person develops his mental faculties that allow him to move profitably from dependence to independence. There should be the realisation that there is nothing inherently weak, exploitative, or intimidating about either 'dependence' and 'independence'; they are simply terms that designate levels of commitment and connectivity within a relationship that contribute to the furtherance of a certain goal. After all, there is nothing wrong with saying that one was 'dependent' on parents for financial support during one's pursuit of a graduate degree at a university. It is through a series of *successive events* that one attains control over life and self in order to ultimately reach authentic fulfilment. Separation from the group in order to become a competent, healthy, disciplined, and independent person—the realm in which the term 'individuation' is ordinarily cognised—is only the most noticeable aspect of the process, not the result.

Thus, the degree of independence in life increases with the extent to which we move outward, breaking with forms found within the family of origin to establish our own habits, to associate with trustworthy people, to obtain the right education and career, and to live with activities we find agreeable. In this matrix, the 'individual' is formed by the interaction of certain forces, such as that which come from personality, family, community, religion, and culture. These areas must be examined by every person in relation to their own particular process of individuation.

However, research indicates that the *initial* desire for contact with other people comes not from social environment, but from the attribute of extroversion, which is largely genetically determined (see Sporer 2010A). The appetite for autonomy is influenced to an extent by home life, friends, peers, teachers, and other persons within an individual's local social sphere, but the *innate* desire for independence is determined for the most part by the level of extroversion, is a genetic and, for the most part, an unalterable trait. Innate shyness might be overridden due to the persistent prodding of siblings and parents. As conducive this is to meeting parental expectations, it has a negative impact on individuation processes, because one cannot believe that one is totally independent, unless one obeys a fundamental internal principle governing the need for mental and emotional intimacy. How the individual and other people deal with extroversion affects perceptions of future life.

Nonetheless, complete congruence between temperament and situation is not always desirable. When the life track conforms generally to innate strengths, there are no real challenges, and there is consequently no learning, as one does not confront situations that are unusual and intriguing; advancement psychologically clearly demands new understandings about oneself. Hence, managing challenges in life are an important part of creating an identity, and the family should give the individual the means to meet the varied difficulties he could encounter in school, business, and social venues.

In essence, the moral principles one learns early in life must change a person's inherent tendencies, as the knowledge of human nature must turn certain innate forces of personality to the right orientation, if there is to be success and true accomplishment in life. The family environment figures prominently in this process, for here parents know their children's innate tendencies, and thus can assist in shaping their thinking into productive forms. Of course, no one can force a child to think in a certain way, but one can certainly make clear to the child the errors in his thinking by both pointing out the negative consequences, and by elucidating a better way of thinking.

Every person's individuation process must begin somewhere, it must have a platform on which it is based, and that platform will likely be the family into which one was born, containing one's parents and siblings. Consequently, as the household of childhood acts as a training ground, platform, or launchpad for larger social relations, family relations will often determine the ease of forming and maintaining relationships. The relationships which family members have with one another, and the way that those members judge materialism, can determine an individual's 'attractiveness' as marriage candidate. What happens in childhood might therefore ultimately have an impact on relationships, especially intimate ones. When desired patterns of association are frustrated, self-image is damaged, which in turn increases the need to prove one's independence.

From the foregoing, we infer that one should not lose sight of one-on-one relations between family members, which are more important than group-to-one relations in establishing a pattern of individuation. These one-to-one interactions provide experience with developing sympathy for others, and seeking fair and equitable relationships. The only place where this type of group interaction occurs is in the family, for in most other contexts, such as school and playground, the interactions involve attention and activity that are spread out over more than two people.

Direct experiential contact is enduring and powerful. Each person in a child's life takes on one or more roles, who can elucidate ideas concerning sympathy, internal values, equality, justice and improving the community. These values must develop normally in young people, for without them there can be no true 'individual'; the person would have no independent thinking, he would only be the container of whatever social influences he ingested during the course of his life. The family situation is especially useful in defining the moral quality of actions, something that young people have difficulty understanding. Assigning responsibility for behaviour, who does 'good' and who does 'bad', can only be provided within the family household, where there can be explanations by a father or mother who is a respected arbiter, someone who can be trusted to deliver an accurate assessment. Other persons outside the family are largely unknown as to their motivations for judgement, and so cannot be relied upon to substantively educate young people in moral assessment.

The domestic situation in which the individual is raised is the closest to the one which he or she will experience, in his or her own marriage. Thus, the family of childhood can act as a model of married life. For example, a man with positive experiences in the family, especially where he feels that his psychological development is being nurtured, will be eager to form such a household himself. In other, situations, family can act as an anti-model, where the activities in the household are perceived as serving no useful purpose, other than fulfilling material goals. This materialistic paradigm of life forces a downgrading in classification: The group living within the residence are no longer a 'family', but merely a 'household'. Acrimonious relations within the family can impel the younger members to leave home early in search of peace and a better 'family', although without the support of older authority figures, poor career choices and inappropriate relations with the opposite sex are likely to occur. Other relations within the household of origin also have indirect and direct effects on one's overall psychological well-being.

The structure of the family, meaning the organisation of the responsibilities and activities of members, is also a significant factor in affecting psychological development. In those households where the parents and children see the family as a private entity focussed on promoting the individuation of its members, parents will then be both guardians and friends to their children. But in those cases where family members perceive 'family' only as a socially determined economic 'unit', then parents will tend to be authoritarian. We can see that in large families, and others where parents demand a militaristic-type adherence to chores and assignments, there is a tendency to produce persons who are inflexible and selfish, whose lone desire in life is to serve only 'me'. Coming from a large family can make the individual feel only like 'one of the kids', not a separate personality; one needs to leave to establish his own identity if one is to avoid loneliness and depression. But, there are also potential rewards in such a situation. A large family gives the individual the opportunity to develop skills in dealing with people, increasing his confidence. Appreciation for the lessons learned in social behaviour might not be forthcoming if crowding, arguing and other 'people' problems are not resolved.

It is evident that there are households where good relations exist between parents and children, because the former have conscientiously nurtured the mental development of the latter. These parents impart positive values, and assist in the development of the child's moral thinking. Other family members, such as aunts, uncles, cousins, etc, might have an prominent role in helping children through the maturation process. Boys and girls both react more favourably to specific input from family members who are within a particular age group, since different age groups have their own concerns and outlook. Nevertheless, closeness between family members is significantly affected by a variety of events, such as divorce, death, and emigration. The departure of a mentor can also entail the loss of a role that he or she was elucidating, with the result that the child is impaired in development.

Although social institutions cannot supply the equivalent of parenting in the area of mental development, they can provide information, guidelines, and rules about social behaviour. Hence, moral principles can be provided not just by family, but through larger social dynamics. A person can draw important cues in relation to improving his community, which can lead him to become pro-social and sympathetic, desirous of protecting rights of others because he is sensitised to the living conditions of his fellow citizens. In this case, however, reasoning must be at least moderately developed, and the person must also have strongly conceived internal values, and must register emotions in relation to the attainment or rejection of those values. Moral reasoning can affect a person's evaluation of his surroundings, and how well he reasons out his situation in the pursuit of his personal goals. For example, living conditions, including quality of residence, rooms, private space, etc, are an essential issue for everyone's marriage plans. This means that the individuation process is, to an extent, a function of material factors.

The most important sources of moral concepts institutions of education and mass media communication. Education and media access affect social communications concerning living conditions, and these forces alter perceptions of time frame and the relative values of both independence and companionship. One then must decide for oneself how much one's own living situation is similar to others in society, and how would intimate relationships fulfill one's personal goals.[20] If information flow is lower in a society, then people might be less aware of their surroundings, and must depend more on traditional concepts as communicated by their parents. Further, the people in this context possibly confuse their personal situation with the general situation, which indicates perhaps poorer developed mental faculties. We should understand that, in relation to satisfaction with home life, *what the individual believes in many cases to be a personal valuation is really social*; it is not content, but the form of information that often influences decisions, because messages about the 'empowering' independent lifestyle are often the same across industrialised cultures.

However, the interactions between individual, family and outside forces is complex. Obtaining a high level of education is the major focus today in the individuation process, because it is believed that it gives the greatest opportunity to develop intellectual freedom and distinction. Indeed, the most important factor outside the home that influences individuation is that of education, which is usually a product of family relations, mediated by social activities, good grades, and participation in organisations. Success in college seems to be affected more by success in secondary school organised activities, rather than competence in informal, routine, low-value social actions. This underlines again the importance of structure, since young people will become more competent through coordinated, prioritised participation.

It is important to note that the family of origin might have an effect on one's educational plans, which in turn influences personality, since higher education often creates a shift in emphasis on relationship issues. For example, inadequate parenting might leave the development of rational and moral faculties to the inconsistent dynamics usually found in institutional settings. Further, the desire of a person from a poorly integrated family to seek companionship might force him to abandon education plans, and might result in a lower family income and lower status in his own married life. Nonetheless, those who come from better functioning families have faced their own challenges in the education system. Thus, an especially complex issue is the effect that education has on personality and relationships.

Surveying what we have discussed, we can see that the term 'childhood home' has many strong positive associations: It signifies warmth, protection, guardianship, nurturance, safety, training, self-realisation. This 'platform' for individuation truly encompasses many influences, coming from inside and from outside. In modern society, departure from this most conducive environment to a new home is a sign that the individual now seeks to begin his own independent existence, which for most people, after a period of time, leads to marriage and establishing a family of one's own. Although the age at which this happens varies, the general expectation is that it will occur at around 21, so that the person will begin contributing to the economy—a good, bright beginning for the responsible citizen. However, not all leave at the time of official 'maturity'. Some people continue to live in the family home because of cultural influences, some do simply because it is cheaper to do so, and others have complex reasons drawn from personal areas. Clearly, when a person leaves his family, he takes on certain risks, because he no longer enjoys financial support, advice, and emotional assistance. It is, therefore, no surprise that even the 'correct' age of leaving home is based on the legal definitions of adulthood, thus dropping the blame for any problems that develop onto the whole of society. In this case, the responsibility for failure would be 'no one's'.

For the person leaving his home of childhood, the arrangement of social interactions will change, making him cognisant of the role differentials pertinent to family 'egress'. This event involves going from a situation of long-standing stability, to another one much more unfamiliar, and in proportion more uncertain. Only in the case of the military service does society present a structure ready-made for the individual after departure; in all other situations, society encourages egress, but provides no other substantive assistance. The world outside the home lacks definite arrangements that are stable and easily accessible, for young people there are only loose associations.

Accordingly, socialising with friends is no longer a leisurely activity, but a 'labour' that often requires effort and counteracts the idea that the event is pleasurable. Indeed, part of the range of external forces that affect one's desire for companionship, involves recreation or divertissements, which can act as a substitute for marriage or a prelude to it. When the demand is high for a mate, and there are no other acceptable 'dedicated' venues for meeting potential mates, any leisure activity that involves the opposite sex is instrumental. Yet, how much genuine gratification is obtained from such activities, as one would receive from accomplishing clear goals, is open to question.

It is in interest of modern society, however, to create the myth of choice and control, and this is done by erecting barriers between activities, and reducing their cross-influencing effect. Society has created separate 'ritual acts' for each area—recreation, entertainment, friendship meetings, and dating are now distinct entities, each with its own rules. Individuation is hampered, because ritualism discourages personal initiative and solutions. As a result, casual socialising, potentially an excellent source of insight into human behaviour, is encumbered with awkward rules that limit opportunities to observe, and interact with, others without intimidation or commitment.

Thus, the individual must be prepared to make plans for himself after leaving, and to take the risks as well. Traditional thinking was clear about this issue: Any reason to remain living with parents, or to leave to form a new household, is valid so long as it improves the individual's well-being, and the benefits are greater than the costs. When one is not prepared, either intellectually, organisationally, or financially to leave home, then it is undeniable that one will be encumbered by a lack of confidence about the future. This situation does not aid the individuation process because it forces compromises in key areas. If the decision to leave was not his own, the individual will eventually learn his 'liberation' was hollow, and his independence is not authentic. If the decision to leave was self-initiated, and the basis was a lack of love at home, then he will be more likely to rush to another relationship, giving the impression of being responsible whilst still being unprepared. The inability to have close relations with a parent or sibling might prompt a desire for true companionship in marriage that was denied at home. Therefore, one can either be 'fired', or one might 'resign', but in either case one's plans are thwarted, and there is never any genuine autonomy.

As one could claim that there was 'strong' recurrent pressure from parents and others to exit, the responsibility for failure in adult life might partly lie with family members; then again, with few exceptions, no one actually threatens bodily removal, making it more likely that the individual himself is chiefly responsible for his own plight. Accountability often remains amorphous in the modern age, and a critical transitional stage in the individuation process is left unresolved.

Evidence of making an appropriate decision, a correct choice, alone does not indicate a fully formed personality. The whole person must be considered before any judgement can be made about that person's character. It is clear that the individual's level of maturity is directly proportionate to the extent to which he takes responsibility for his actions, and avoids faulting others for decisions that are his alone. An important sign of maturity is found in the resolution of the issue of how the individual perceives the concept of 'independence', that is, of reaching true individual status. By understanding how independence is treated in the childhood family, we can discern the inefficiencies and mistakes in individual development, and so learn where the adjustments need to be made in modern society that will remedy the problems which we have identified. Questions must be asked: Do I need support or can I go it alone? Can security, efficiency, and orderliness be obtained with the help of acquaintances and institutions, or can these aspects only be realised through the cooperation of a spouse? There are no absolute correct answers, except to say that it is self-evidently wrong for one to disregard one's own plans for finding happiness in life. To seek a spouse in order to have find fulfilment is no weakness, but *not* to seek one when one is very much desired is a sign of pusillanimity.

We should be aware that certain common status marker issues, such as staying out late, reducing contact with parents, moving from the parental home, sharing a residence with roommates, etc, were not in the past treated as great 'milestones', and were not as important socially and personally in marriage decisions previously as today, either because their relevance was not highlighted culturally, or there were legitimate substitutes. In the traditional or 'pre-modern' era, the individual could minimise the significance of these issues, and focus more on those matters over which he had greater control, bolstering his self-esteem.

Thus, complex forces affect everyone in the individuation process. European traditions have guaranteed that personal ideals should be discovered (or if necessary, recovered) and implemented without undue pressure from outside factors, individual or institutional. The family has, for centuries, been the place where the individual could secure vital information about the functioning of groups and institutions. Despite the frequent use of modern methods, there is no question that the traditional concept is still valid: The proper place for the learning and development of mechanisms of logic is the home of childhood. Appropriately, the parents have been given the honour of being the great teachers in this noble project, sparking enlightenment in their children through a confluence of *explication* of personal and inherited traditional wisdom, and *exhibition* of acts of honesty, justice, and reciprocity. We must ask: If the family will not provide this critical knowledge about life, then who will?

Let us now study the next step, after a person no longer is under the influence of his family, where he enters into the new role of husband or wife, where the ideas he has obtained from family or community have to be "put to work". We must focus on the effect that external forces have on the individual's ability to integrate the ideas that he has accumulated from early childhood about relationships and family. It is the extent to which a person can coordinate, structure, and blend into a functioning whole the range of ideas at his disposal, rather than the simple knowledge of the ideas themselves, that forms the basis for judging whether he or she has developed into a distinctive, and indeed distinguished, mature person.

Happy they who find the goddess come in moderate might,
sharing with self-restraint in Aphrodite's gift of marriage
and enjoying calm and rest from frenzied passions,
wherein the Love-god, golden-haired, stretches his charmed bow
with arrows twain,
and one is aimed at happiness, the other at life's confusion.
   IPHIGENIA AT AULIS (410 BC), by Euripides (484 BC-406 BC)

Could we dispense with wives, Romans, we would have one nui-
sance less. However, since nature has decreed that we cannot live
very comfortably with them, and without them not at all, we
should look rather to our long-term welfare than to our short-
term pleasure.
   QUINTUS METELLUS NUMIDICUS

Chapter 5

The Integration of Ideas

*D*ynamics, as patterns of force or energy, govern every system in Nature. The dynamics inside the family household, as well as outside of it, must be understood if there can be a fruitful combination of marital with social roles. The family, in both its structure and its interpersonal relations, must be the source of pertinent and relevant wisdom on the workings of society, which the individual will face throughout his life. However, these effects flow down a 'two-way street', and although family will influence the individual's thinking about society, society will also affect perceptions about the family.

Consequently, one's decisions about education, career, and family structure are significantly influenced by the community. Unique conflicts arise from this practise, which does not necessarily affect the individuation process, but which might be exacerbated by stress carried over from work into the home and personal life. Choices related to marriage are also influenced by economic variables, such as the cost of food, clothing, durables, and housing, since conjointly running a household might mitigate financial burdens, and help one reach cultural expectations about standard of living. Hence, it is often seen that when expenses for personal items are high, marriage is early.

Society imposes certain obligations that affect personal views of both independence and companionship. Nevertheless, in order for family to be a viable entity, concerns with status, occupation, social duty, and so forth must effectively and cogently be handled, without submitting to the dominating influence of materialism. Thus, even if many influences come from the culture, all ideas must still be integrated, they must 'work' together, where the individual's goals connect with appropriate resources, and his thinking and beliefs are congruent with each other, and are relevant to the situation at hand, so that challenges can be met effectively and efficiently.

A young person must obtain information of high quality about all important areas of life; parents must assist their children in finding enduring values, and in correcting them when they make the mistake of pursuing goals that are ephemeral, weak, and unhealthy. The interaction between members of the family affects one's sociability; some traits might be less useful in marriage than in economic and business matters, especially in dealing with the requirements of an occupation. A career does not run parallel to family, but interrelates with it. Family and peer relations provide the foundation for one's work life, but the latter can also interfere with fundamental emotional dynamics in relationships. An ignorance of these interrelationships will hinder individuation, as the attributes needed to adjust to the complex situations in life, and progress beyond entanglements, might be absent.

Yet, in the modern era, an absence of constructive relations between parent and child is common. Growing up in a home without moral guidance does not dissuade people from marrying, and indeed seems to encourage them to do so, probably because they want a family that will satisfy their unrequited requests for affection, comfort, and security. It is more likely that the desire for continued assistance in psychological development will motivate men and women to *hasten* marriage in relation to deficiencies in the family of childhood, such a departure of mentors. The lack of development of internal values makes young people seek others for guidance about how to react to various social situations. In other words, the absence of appropriate parental guidance and advice, for whatever reason, bestows upon marriage a *compensatory* function, and this will cause some to marry quickly so as to partake of something truly 'special', that they cannot achieve in any other type of social context. It is clear that the departure of a mentor and role model can hinder the individuation process, because personality development is not completed, and dependence on others might be necessary.

A shortage of advice and support, in addition to deficient attention paid to emotional needs, was often in the past attributed to living in a large family, or losing a parent due to death. A person from a large family can simultaneously be less desirable as a marriage partner, but also be more desiring of companionship. There is little doubt that these factors even today continue to influence motivations in the search for a companionate partner. However, additional factors must be present that would account for the current widespread paucity of maturity in young people. The most likely culprit would be the *parental abnegation of responsibility*, though this is far more difficult to measure than death or family size. Therefore, we can at this point refer to the high divorce and separation rates in the Western world as strong evidence not only of conflict between spouses, but also of failure to provide relevant, structured, long-term instruction and guidance of children. With so much thoughtlessness, coarseness, and selfishness in abundance, no one should marvel at the disturbing prevalence of marital conflict, and the general animosity and 'meanness' between men and women.

Family disruption is especially a critical influence when the individual is temperamentally disposed to insecurity. Therefore, a person growing up in a home with inadequate support and instruction has a tendency to behave unwisely, being more likely to leave home early, less likely to finish high school, less likely to attend college, less likely to deal competently with peers. He or she requires assistance in the self-development process and is likely to date and marry early. Despite this desire to marry early, the individual might not be mentally prepared for marriage. Indeed, such a decision demonstrates a victory of emotion over reason, which is not desirable under any circumstances. Yet, in the pursuit of money, one has to be a success in one's career, and often, if one is not willing to be 'tough' and inflexible, one cannot achieve a high standard of living. When the individual is successful in a career, he finds he can then marry and start family life earlier because he has the financial wherewithal to bring these components together, but it is precisely the lifestyle that has bestowed this opportunity on him that denies him ease in finding a marriage partner, and denies him the time to savour this relationship.

Hence, both the events of early life in the family of origin, and the events of career in young adulthood are responsible for how the individual puts together, into an integrated format, ideas concerning marriage. The lack of proper development in understanding the positive roles of sympathy, values, equality, justice, community does not necessarily impede success in career, where the most important factors might be ambition, perseverance, even ruthlessness, but they do have a negative bearing in intimate relationships. Rigidity in personality due to the demands of a career can lead to poorly structured friendships, and this might delay marriage. Ironically, even though a person has poor skills in relation to intimacy, in some cases he might still forge an early marriage through false 'charm'. Yet, we must look at the situation from a different perspective. Some people who lack proper intellectual and moral development will delay marriage, because they are more meticulous in temperament, and are prepared to wait to find just the right person, precisely in order not to disturb the ideal 'specialness' of this relationship. Companionship in adulthood is assigned a higher value, although so high in some cases that the individual takes great time to decide on a marriage partner.

Experiences in the family of childhood can cover a wide range, capable of producing very different types of personas who carry with them impressions that extend far into adult life. We have seen two antithetical examples. Simply speaking, either one is flexible, with a low standard of living and earlier marriage, or one is uncompromising, with a high standard of living and late marriage. If personality were the only factor affecting marriage prospects, then this principle could be accepted. However, that is not the case, as other factors, such as education, are also important. The individuation process is given great attention in either case of early or late marriage, but with early marriage, the process is endangered by an injudicious choice of a marriage partner for the sake of continuity, from the home of childhood to the home of adulthood. If a person marries too early, then there is the possibility of over-dependence due to stunted development of critical faculties. Further, when reliance turns to over-dependance, then any kind of independent behaviour becomes impossible to achieve. As a result, earlier marriage might result in an inability to negotiate potentially profitable opportunities, as well as an awkwardness in navigating around insurmountable obstacles. If one has difficulty in simply getting ideas across, one has little hope of making genuine progress in reaching an intimate level of discourse. On that ground, it is thought that obstacles must be 'removed' through simplification and subjectivisation of standards. This strategy, with its tampering of critical conceptual domains, is dangerous to say the least.

As we know, restrictions on life choices are common, and the individual does not have a free hand in many areas. Certain ancient demands, peculiar to Western cultures, are well-known to most people, who are expected to attain a higher standard of living than the previous generation, with future income being added to an inheritance (if any) and personal savings. Intellectual and physical capital in turn is to be passed on to the next generation, who will have the same demands made of them. 'Economics' in a larger sense, that is, the functioning of various markets, has always played a role in the decision to marry, with inheritance, occupation, male-female ratios, and mortality rates being of significance.

Thus, external factors over which the individual does not have as much control as over the family are also crucial to an individual's life. Things in nature, however, do not always operate according to well-understood principles, and unpredictability in status and accidents of birth create tension. As a way of reducing this tension, the cultures of the Western world have assisted the individual by establishing a number of milestones, such as education, career, marriage, and parenthood, and connecting them with what a variety of life-paths. We should stress that these were general guidelines, and not social dictates. The individual has traditionally followed a course where he would grow up as a member of a household; obtain academic qualifications; establish himself in an occupation; save money; search for an available partner; marry; raise children; inherit his parents' holdings; pass on his resources to the next generation. Each step is, to a greater or lesser degree, dependent on the others, although modern authorities often tend to treat each component in isolation. We would expect each step to increase responsibility and gratification, but general cultural principles sometimes exceed an individual's competence. Whatever the personal timeline of events, individuals in the past stood a good chance of reaching their life goals because they had the maturity to *envision* the road ahead.[21]

Modern cultures, although concerned to an extent about individuation, adjust society's focus more narrowly on the career area, and so converge attention on the material sphere. To a large extent, a community's standard of living is now also international, and it would appear that the general dynamic across the Western world is to marry but only if there is the following set of factors:

» consistent, steady employment
» relatively high personal income
» at least a moderate concentration of wealth

These three 'rules' worked well for our ancestors. However, a simplistic, preoccupying focus on these factors might significantly impede individuation, because they then *displace* other issues of importance such as beliefs, attitudes, disposition and tastes. Because of their interrelationship, their repeated appearance in analyses, and the emphasis that society places on them, three requirements—employment, high income and moderate wealth—can be considered the material 'golden rules' governing the traditional conception of marriage. In the present day, these rules have become the merely 'guidelines'. A person might avoid marrying because he believes he is guilty of not fulfilling one or more of these requirements, but then he risks permanently crippling the individuation process; the force of society's 'ideal happy family' based on *material considerations* is so powerful that it appears to overshadow personal emotional and psychological needs. Material considerations of the modern era are manifold and confusing, and so establishing rules is difficult. This is why, it is difficult, at the present time, for a person to explain what they personally consider 'steady employment' or 'adequate income'. Their 'rule' will waver and change from over time, fluctuate according to the situation or who is asking the question. Once again, external forces determine personal 'belief'.

Without knowledge of the limitations of a particular society, based on a realistic, sober assessment, there can be no possibility of putting together a viable plan for accomplishing goals in life. At some point, the individual must develop a realisation of a 'rule' in life, a *sine qua non*, a goal which must be met before another goal can be accomplished. As we have seen, modern people have very poor access to such solid, clear thinking.

We can see from the foregoing that social factors exist that can, in fact, overpower the dynamics of individuation. The *concept of family* is consequently weak and unintegrated, because many people find themselves drawing their experiences about 'family' from unrewarding and disjointed situations. These situations, such as remaining single and unmarried or living at home with parents, are not the result of individual preference, but rather are derived from conditions present in the modern industrial urbanised economy. A situation involving unemployment, low educational attainment, unsociable demeanor, divorce, or mental illness often forces people to make choices about their life path that they do not want. In the past, however, it was possible for people to live alone or with a spouse in spite of these social conditions, and conversely, people could continue to live with their own parents without necessarily having any such difficulties. The implication of these observations is that persons in the current time who return to, or remain with, their family of origin not only suffer from inadequate individual development, but are victims to a certain extent of a society that no longer has functioning *compensatory* mechanisms.

The way in which outside influences is generally treated today invites the idea that the individuation process was better in the past, because external influences were minimised. When the prospects for a good economy are not there, especially in relation to the three golden 'rules', men and especially women are not likely to marry.

We can conclude that the integration of ideas about family is negatively affected, to a considerable extent, by a host of issues. It is easy to observe when summarising the influences on the decision to marry, such as in the above paragraphs, the pitfalls inherent in modern industrialised society, where the demands of ideology, school, community, career, family, and friends, challenge the individual from all sides. Yet, people tend to overemphasise these obvious social demands, and neglect more subtle but vital factors. This imbalance is often seen in choices relating to independence, where poor decisions can lead to problems that make one unable to reach the twin goals of material and emotional satisfaction. Independence concepts then mediate between the two; people become wrapped up in areas that take away valuable resources, as in the case where one chooses to take a high paying career, thus gaining independence, but also reducing marriage choices because of long hours and inflexible behaviour. On the other hand, by not paying much attention to independence, one could decide to seek 'love' and marry early, yet this restricts educational and job opportunities and income. To look at it another way, the level of independence in one's life regulates the flow of energy between material and emotional satisfaction: Open it up too much, and energy flows too much to one side; close it down too much, and energy flows too much to the other. Decisions about autonomy must be made first, or in conjunction with decisions about career, materialism, and companionship.

When reviewing all the evidence that pertains to the material aspects of securing a family household, one comes to the unavoidable conclusion that, whereas in the past the tendency was for men and women to worry about physical issues relating to marriage as a result of concern for themselves *and* their partners, in our day, this concern is only *self-centred*. Material matters are, of course, no less important today than in the past, but are often sought with *only* one's own interests in mind; this relates to the situations before, during, and after courtship.

This is not to say that traditionally, economic issues lacked significance. Money in the past could not make love, but too much or too little money could destroy it, or at least seriously damage the showing of affection. The customs of our ancestors could not be clearer: Marry before rigid habits set in, but not so early as to prevent reaching a minimal level of emotional self-sufficiency. In addition, the more discipline and hard work one puts into finding a spouse, the less effort must be expended within marriage.

Today, the traditional 'timeline' is no longer followed, which is, in and of itself, not necessarily fatal to the cause of personal happiness, but it is troubling that so many people lay out their life course thinking that any combination of factors is as navigable as any other.[22] In particular, family life in modern society has been discounted in influence, to the point where the concept of 'family' is not considered an issue worthy of ratiocination. If the average person of the modern age abandons traditional ideas, and tries to understand human nature using his own intellectual mechanisms, then he will come to incorrect and possibly dangerous observations if his mental abilities are poorly developed. Naturally, moral issues, the set of rules that creates a balance between individual and community interests, override general material and pragmatic principles. However, there is overwhelming evidence that the lack of moral reasoning capabilities has caused a shift in the balance between individual needs and communal needs, with greater emphasis on the latter.

In these cases where materialism is the guiding force, the quality of the relationship between men and women is the result of chance factors. Competence in social evaluation alone is not enough to secure a happy marriage, for there must also be sensitivity and solicitude, features which come from deep inside the individual psyche. Thus, we see instances where families with higher levels of connectivity produce competent individuals who are capable of achieving notable career success, but incompetent in attending to the needs of their relationships. Standard of living goals might be reached, but at a cost to the relationship. Moreover, tension arises when rates of maturity are mismatched in a relationship, resulting in a non-equal association containing a 'leader' and a 'follower'. This situation is exacerbated by other discrepancies, such as in the case where one spouse earns wages higher than the other. Of course, in a truly companionate relationship, where both the man and woman are mature and considerate, there is no overall 'leader' or 'follower', even if society does press for such ranking.[23]

On the whole, society's suggested approaches to accomplishment have never been overly friendly, but with deft handling the interconnections between various components can be successfully managed. It appears that for many people the milestones found in education, family, community, and work can all be made without serious problems, demonstrating that great individual control over life is still feasible. The truth is that, in European cultures, the life path was never rigid, and alterations could be made without opprobrium, but *it was essential that the individual understood the limitations of society and nature,* and this is precisely where the modern citizen fails. Fulfilment is not necessarily possible where forces foreign and antithetical to the individuation process are ignored. For example, unemployment, disputes with parents, and burdensome work rules might seem to be issues unrelated to finding a marriage partner, yet they do in fact have a consequence on relationships through their ability to alter the *intention to cooperate, sacrifice, and abide.* It should be evident that people can, with effort, modify their life pathways, but not certain interactions and connections which are essentially unalterable. The creation of the pathway must, therefore, take into account these 'points of interest', much as a traveller would plan a route that avoids cities, mountains, and uncrossable rivers.

Love and family are still important in our generation, but negative expectations about what might arise in relationships, from early adulthood onwards, reinforced by actual negative experiences, now loom so large as to displace traditional principles. The effects of arguments, cheating, lying, breakups cannot be easily dismissed, and after a period of time begin to contribute to a 'counter-concept' of family. Yet, the average person depends on the opposite sex more than ever for assistance in cobbling together a workable view of the ways of society, perhaps obtaining in this way life's only psychological satisfaction, but not so much as to renounce key elements of autonomy. If, as is often the case, the relationship itself is poorly constructed, most available time is spent trying to repair breeches, and individuation is cast to the wind.

Ea libertas est qui pectus purum et firmum gestitat;
aliae res obnoxiosae nocte in obscura latent
Freedom is having a pure and dauntless heart; all else is slavery
and lies hidden in darkness

    QUINTUS ENNIUS (239-169 BC)

Miraris, cum tu argento post omnia ponas,
si nemo praestet quem non merearis amorem?
Can you wonder, when you rank everything after your money,
that no one renders you the love which you do not earn?

    QUINTUS HORATIUS FLACCUS (65-8 BC)

Chapter 6

Pursuing an Elusive Image of Fulfilment

*E*xistence within a civilised society can offer many rewards, and possibly there is no greater compensation for effort than that found in the family. Our investigations into family life have shown, time and again, that the 'ingredients' to such a successful, enduring intimate relationship are cooperation, consideration, and sacrifice. Of course, these terms have synonyms and can be expanded upon, but the fundamental meanings should be well understood by anyone whose mind is open to the potential gratification that family life can bestow. We have also seen how the elementals of these meanings have been embedded into European culture, and can therefore be discovered through an examination of history and society. The ways in which a person can share intimacy with another person must ultimately be determined by every individual, utilising knowledge gained from his own observations and participation, as well as from collective experience.

For the just idealist, that is, someone whose interests and outlook are approximately similar to the ideals contained in traditional European culture, principles can be deduced which become dependable guidelines for reaching goals in the areas of marriage, education, standard of living, and career. Therefore, we find we are fortunate that certain principles that go into the creation of ideals about relationships can be elucidated; these principles exist in a realm beyond a particular culture, place, or time. Nonetheless, it is up to the individual to make proper use of these principles within his own life, and to take full responsibility for the consequences that might occur from their implementation.

Our ancestors understood these issues, and they believed that to achieve fulfilment, it was foolish for society to limit the individual to only one course. Many known roads—some longer, some shorter—led home to life's spiritual contentment, but many other unknown paths, equally if not more useful, could be discovered. Still, the greatest care must be exercised in forging these new routes to happiness; the individual's intellectual mechanisms must be sound, objectivity and sensitivity must be strongly developed. From the well-signposted trails of traditions, rules, and customs, modern man emerges in the wilderness of supposed self-realisation. He proudly hikes alone, for a time happily follows his own course, yet realises his vulnerability. Among the few important items he carries in his rucksack is the personal 'treasure map' of fulfilment, containing the milestones that indicate achievement of a type has been attained. For these riches his desire never weakens, but successfully finding them requires immense sacrifices. In spite of our traveller's determination to bring into reality his strongly felt ideas about family, it would be wrong to think all other dreams, hopes, and goals will be extinguished in order to achieve it, for there are other attractions in the land that draw his attention.

This wanderlust is perhaps not unexpected in an age which so strongly recommends migration as a way to satisfy goals relating to education and work. However, this mentality, encouraging as it does through the cutting of ties and looseness of association, reinforces immature concepts of independence. The modern cultural ethos of independence is analogous to a childhood belief, where individuals expect freedom and love whenever and wherever they find it necessary. Yet, unlike many other situations in life, this childhood 'fantasy' can become a reality, but only on a limited scale, and only when one constructs it properly. The 'whenever' and 'wherever' of desire must occur within the confines of the family household, and if one is able to obtain emotional gratification at least within that context, then one will be less fanatical about receiving rewards in the larger world outside. The 'secret' wisdom pertaining to marital happiness is not really secret at all, in the sense that some great treasure trove of information is deliberately kept from view by forces unknown. Wisdom is, in reality, the 'gold' that needs to be disentangled from the mass of suppositions, irrelevancies, and falsehoods that make up the 'dirt' of any situation. Although there are malign persons who want to stop us from *searching* for the truth, the struggle primarily is to force ourselves to keep on pursuing the truth, in spite of dead ends and wrong turns.

Thus, love cannot be measured using contrived social indicators, rather it is in the *enduring quality*, the reliability of the relationship, that is important. We can see why such a relationship can be likened to a precious metal such as gold—because it durable, valuable, and rare. Since this love comes through relying on one another, giving and accepting trust, it cannot be accomplished if people are duplicitous. The strength of the pair is ultimately dependent on the strength and resiliency of the individuals who make up the unit, and both husband and wife must have the courage to be honest with themselves and with each other. The most powerful relationship can occur only between people who ready to join together in a unique partnership, one which cannot be broken. We can say that this union of man and woman has a *singularity of purpose*. Without being esoteric, we can say our ancestor's concept of 'singularity' simply meant a relationship where conversation and activity are unhindered, and where ideas usually find agreement and support. *It does not necessarily mean having the same temperament, personality, or background.* Two people might ostensibly be quite dissimilar, but still get along superbly because they possess comparable views on the fundamental issues in life.

Actually, this closeness can be so great that another person becomes, in essence, a part of one's own mind, which still retains its independent thought processes and knowledge, but can relate to a companion's thoughts and actions. In such a case, ideas are often anticipated, and husbands and wives often know what the other will say and do. The existence within the institution of *connubium* should be as easy as living alone, but with all the advantages of cooperative support, love, and affection.

The great emotional repose that beckons people to live with one another in marriage is predicated on a certain *effortlessness* in experience, which is in turn based on achieving a singularity of mind. Note, however, that there might be great effort in creating such a marital situation, but once reached, there is an ease which more than makes up for the previous expenditures. Our ancestors understood this principle: One must expend resources to build one's household, before one can live comfortably in it. Indeed, if marriage simply promised a marginally 'better' way of life, it would have very little power to persuade us to make a major sacrifice of personal resources. There must be a reward that far outweighs the expense. We can find solace in the very old saying, that true love will always prevail over all tests. Although a couple might have problems with finances, relatives, occupation, and so on, the relationship will not only last but function well, because neither can think of having any other life except with each other. This is not merely a notion, but the ideal of family brought to life, a rare example of a truly glorious social arrangement upon which we can cast all the light of inspection we wish on it, and it will not wither.

We have in this work given the impression that, far from being dejected about the difficulties in marriage, one should be sanguine about the benefits that this venerable institution has to offer the individual. More than ever, the inhabitants of the modern world are seeking emotional satisfaction from their relationship, whilst emphatically refusing to make the sacrifices that are necessary to preserve that relationship. Men and women have drifted further apart in really understanding each other's elemental needs. Effective social intercourse is even more important in married life than in other dyadic relationships, and success in this regard makes necessary speech that is articulate, plain, forthright, and thoughtful. But that is only one aspect of family life, as actions are just as important as words. All the various components that we have described as 'ingredients' to the successful marital relationship must be considered *integral*, that is, essential to completeness and lacking nothing essential.

There is no doubt that if the average relationship is to improve, then general attitudes in relation to love and affection must be modified. But for this to happen, the very process of individuation must change. Accordingly, what needs to happen is a fundamental shift in the individual *weltanschauung*, i.e., view of the world. A drastic turnabout, so to speak, must occur that breaks with current forms of thinking. Let us examine this more closely.

In the past, the process of individuation was understood as a form of *internal discovery*, and external factors were only for instrumental use in this great effort. Men and women had what could be called an *afferent* attitude to life, meaning to move inward, as opposed an *efferent* attitude, to move outward. The individual lived with an enthusiasm, one could perhaps call it a drive, for moving towards a centre, a place where all forces coalesce. As a powerful symbolic image, the home is a place where spouse, children, relatives, possessions, accomplishments are all together, defended and secure.

In this regard, one thinks of the changes that occurred in a Christian symbol seen in many European cathedrals and churches, that of the maze. The individual's path was usually an unbroken progression *inwards* towards the *centre*, where God or Godliness was located. The length of the paths might differ, some might be more tortuous than others, but all eventually led to Heaven. The process of discovery was aimed at finding the one Truth, with the external activities of business and community only a means to an end. The goal of life was spiritual—to take to heart whatever was good from others in order to achieve *perfection* of mind and spirit. In was in the era of 'unified Europe', during the so-called Middle Ages, Renaissance, Baroque, and Rococo, when the intellectuals and artists of different nations could openly praise and advance each other's achievements. There was no obsession with patriotism, and thus no fear of being 'belittled' by foreigners, for all men of refined character looked to achieve much more profound aims than promoting the basest common instincts of mankind.

However, after the establishment of the modern mentality about social order, when the 'working man' was the new hero whose way of life had to be sanctified, literally freed from sin and purified, the 'truth' became the reflection of popular opinion; in other words, the means *became* the ends. Even certain theologians promoted this new mentality, where the concept of perfection was denigrated, despite Christ Himself demanding that all men should seek perfection. Hence, the modern period needlessly fomented materialistic and nationalistic divisions of all kinds, and it is not surprising that the definition of 'greatness' became based on the rules of money, power, commerce, and class. In such a milieu, the 'ceiling' of accomplishment was much lowered, where the object of life was merely to attain the *pinnacle* of status or rank, even if it involved stupidity, ruthlessness, or treachery.

These concepts, of promoting the common man and not the ideal man, of seeking to please the masses and not sanctify the Spirit, began even before the Industrial Age. We see this in the symbolic realm, that after the introduction of Protestant modifications to traditional ideas, the conception of the maze was radically altered, with the individual moving *outwards* from the centre, guided by a thin line or tether to God, who was located *outside* the system.[24] Perhaps it is not surprising that Protestantism can neither envisage the Divinity inside the maze of life, nor even see the Godhood as the ultimate goal of enquiry.

From the security of knowing that one inexorably was proceeding towards a single goal, a oneness at the centre of the maze (as within the structured life that the Roman Catholic Church offered), modern man, intoxicated by the possibilities the 'new economy' had to offer, committed himself to move outwards from a secure centre towards an unknown region. In reality, there is a mix of endogenous and exogenous factors that goes into the decision to leave the familiar confines of one's environment: An innate desire for independence; the wish for a better family life or a surrogate family; work-related requirements; educational demands; political demands. Yet, in none of these areas do we see the development of mind or spirit as the ultimate goal. The tedious, albeit certain, journey that took men to God and salvation was transformed into an exciting and dangerous exploration of what lay outside of their 'system'.

In the new schema, the sum total, the 'fulfilment', of one's existence was to be found in some new and better community, family, career, or government, but yet far away from one's place of birth, or family of origin, in the far reaches of the nation, perhaps beyond the edge of the world. There was little to offer the traveller comfort or security. Hence, in this iconography, we see mankind's great struggle to 'come home' to security and love turn into a very different theme, that of a restlessness to 'leave home', for a chance to become 'King of the World'. Strength no longer lay in the safety of the household and family, but in breaking out from a home that for some reason was now a trap. As men moved outwards to explore, the home, whilst never losing its ideal form, gradually faded into one of many places where one could merely hang one's hat.

The modern man or woman has made it clear that they have a self-centred agenda which primarily seeks to make up for the deficiencies brought on by upbringing, education, and career. It is thought that love can be 'forced', so that no great sacrifice or forethought is necessary. We can see this attitude in the nuances of terminology. In modern parlance, one might say that, one 'obtains intimacy from' another person, whereas traditional syntax would have used the construction, one is 'intimate with' another person. Thus, we see within these grammatical forms evidence of parallelism: In the same way a person 'obtains' some pecuniary or physical compensation in a materialistic transaction, that person 'obtains' emotional gratification in an intimate 'transaction'. Both scenarios imply that a simple *quid pro quo* is sufficient to bring satisfaction, and perhaps with some artful deceit, a large return can be gotten through but little investment. Not surprisingly, many people are of the opinion that a lasting, beneficial intimate relationship can be procured even if the man and woman are self-absorbed, aloof, and uncooperative. This peculiarly modern idea—that with artifice and cleverness, anything that a person wants, even love, can be 'gotten' by merely making a small 'payment'— is not only unfounded, it is irrational. Indeed, the myth of unlimited personal power has been raised almost to an article of faith in certain nations where insecurity over solidarity has been prevalent, such as America.

In this madly (and maddeningly) materialistic world, people start with the idea that both true love and material pleasure can be had simultaneously, but then abandon this to focus more on satisfying the body, and not the spirit. They build careful illusions about their 'lovers'. Eventually the illusion is shattered, sometimes as they approach middle age, and the dream has to be reconstructed. There are many recriminations, but hardly any self-examination. 'Expert' help is sought, and after some reassurances people go on thinking that true love can finally be achieved at some cost. Popular external sources of information about the modern dilemma are also for the most part useless. Media representations focus more on 'plots' and ignore characters, and as a result, the motivic energy in a play or film seeks to justify the end result, not the means to attain it. Further, the end result, the 'true love' we are supposedly seeing before our eyes, is almost without exception only an echo of the ideal.

After these disappointments, people might have to alter their time frame, but not their ideals, because they are too precious to discard. Maybe career, friends, fame, money, possessions are not as important as once thought, but one will eventually 'have it all'. These delusions last a lifetime, and for many couples a sort of accordion effect governs their actions: They run to each other, full of promises and hopes, and then when business calls they run away from each other, promising not to be away for too long.

Thus, many people continue to hold a concept of family, wherein they firmly believe in the *possible existence* of a considerate, honest, and mutually fulfilling relationship with a person of the opposite sex. Most people are quite capable of filling deficiencies in their lives by establishing intimate relationships with the opposite sex; these relationships can make up for the many shortfalls and lapses in sustenance and advice that occur in other social settings. Paradoxically, however, they *themselves* do not ever experience the authentic realisation of the concept, instead spending their whole lives buried in worldly matters and business, and never achieving any emotional balance. They complain long and loud about their inability to find 'a good man' or a 'good woman', but habitually underinvest their resources to improve themselves, and wastefully pursue activities that only bring about temporary pleasure.

Although people will do the most selfish and inane things, they go on hoping that their vision, forged in childhood, will one day come true, by giving realisation to the concept of family. It might be three marriages, several children, and innumerable heartaches later, but the dream, they desperately hope, will be realised. The possibility exists that most people will come to understand the foolishness in such a course, as it should be self-evident that no person must be a slave to fads, trends, or mass delusion. Despite the prevalence of negative behaviours, it is fair to say that the *ideal of love* will never die, either in personal life, or in some collective sphere. This in itself is a positive characteristic within human nature, but it does not overcome the critical error that lies in the *conceptualisation* of the ideal. There are indeed true 'idealists' who have a strongly felt archetype of the perfect relationship that they envision in their mind, and just as importantly, who take the appropriate steps to stimulate this *tableau vivant* into action upon the stage of real life. Yet, in the modern landscape there are many hazards for idealists, who constantly struggle to come out into the light of day from under the shadow of Society. No matter how conscientiously an individual seeks to privately build up his own life, groups and institutions make their own complex demands. As a result, marriage is now dragged out into public view to be moulded into a shape that does not interfere with the more important activities of gaining money, possessions, promotions, titles, and awards. Resistance to these forces is possible, but requires inner strength.

We have seen in this work that the concept of family is created with difficulty in the modern age, as various impediments limit the development of moral vision and long-term thinking. When such weaknesses in thinking emerge, the most critical mechanisms used in assessing responsibility—such as empathy, justice, reciprocity—are constrained. Research has provided the formidable evidence that weakness in reasoning capabilities is common in Western populations, and it is likely that they will not much improve as they progress through adulthood. As can be seen in observations of everyday life, it is very difficult to change the components of character. What a person 'is', in a moral sense, at age 18, he is likely to be at age 30, 45, or 70. His behaviour might change, depending on the situation, but his *concerns about the needs, condition, motivations, and status of other people,* are not likely to change. Hence, if a person is willing to lie and cheat in adolescence, he will be willing to do so in later life, even if his behaviour has, from the perspective of other people, been honest. Social forces often will limit selfish and immoral attitudes, but there is little that can change the attitudes themselves.

From the foregoing, it becomes apparent that *a clear concept of family is necessary,* one that transforms a household, from merely a collection of persons, into a healthy, solid base from which individuality can naturally emerge. Accordingly, it is of the greatest importance that the mental and emotional faculties of young people are properly developed within an environment that surrounds them with positive examples of one-to-one interactions. If this is accomplished, by the time they reach the age of 21, they will be capable of turning into reality their own personal concept of family. Along with this focussed development of the powers of the mind, young people should be consistently and regularly reminded that their talents should only be used for constructive purposes, even if this clashes with social trends or popular opinion. In this way, the importance of social status based on simplistic material premisses is minimised. They will come to understand that only a true *individual,* with his own independent, original thoughts, ideals, beliefs, and plans can gain genuine respect from others, and find contentment in life.

To not follow these precepts entails many difficulties for people and society, who must endure incompetent relationships within the family household. But there is an even greater loss, for the loss of individuality means a loss of human character. The individualism of a human being is the greatest surety that the dignity of Man will continue to be respected. The individual would truly be nothing without dignity, and he must do whatever necessary to preserve it. If this principle were the main guide in modern culture, there is no doubt that concept of family life, as found in European history tradition, would be treated with the utmost respect. War, famine, and plague are all horrors, but horrors that in the final analysis can be withstood, for they come from the outside, leaving the individual dignity intact. Betrayal of supposed 'loved ones' comes from one's own weakness, and as such affects both the inside and the outside, the personal and cultural. Hence, once dignity is destroyed, there can be no honour or grace or forgiveness.

All told, it would appear that the greatest misery that men and women can create are what they make for each other. In spite of this, we can rest assured that genuine, pure love can always remain viable in some, perhaps remote sector of mankind's existence, available and ready to deliver the greatest joy to those who can understand what it takes to achieve it. Never has mankind wanted companionship so desperately as today, but never has he sabotaged so many of his efforts to achieve it. Nonetheless, the old wisdom as preserved by European cultural traditions will never be eradicated, and this can still provide the essential principles that can guide modern men and women to consummate their ideals.

Notes

1 Eisenberg et al. (1991), p 854.

2 Eisenberg et al. (1991), p 856-857.

3 Speicher 1992.

4 Boyes & Allen 1993.

5 Muram et al. 1992. This study found that girls aged 14 to 17 who have had a non-marital pregnancy were relatively unconcerned about moral restraints. Further, they were relatively unconcerned about the impact of their current relationships on their own or a future husband's feelings. They were also more likely to see soap operas and romance novels as reflecting real life, and more likely to become aroused to erotic scenes in films. Soap operas and erotic films often feature self-centred activities where moral thinking has no role, and the main goal is immediate sensual gratification. A person without regard for morals would not only find the themes acceptable in these genres, but would also have her own views reinforced.

6 Bar-Yam et al. 1980.

7 Weisheit et al. 1982.

8 Schab 1991.

9 Christopher 1988.

10   Chadwick & Heaton 1992, Table E1-4, p 139.

11   One suspects that even parents somehow know that they
     have not delivered the guidance and affection that their
     children need when they tolerate and even encourage
     early dating. Outwardly, they fear their boy or girl is
     somehow socially 'flawed' if they are not socialising with
     the opposite sex by an early age. However, the truth might
     be that parents do not so much fear what society thinks,
     but fear what they will think of themselves as parents.
     That unloved children often turn out to be rebellious and
     deviant is understood by everyone, but no one appreciates
     this more poignantly than parents who are guilty of with-
     holding affection. Hence, they privately wish that someone
     else will give their children what they have been unwilling
     or unable to do, before it is too late. Perhaps a boyfriend
     or girlfriend can bring a meaning to their child's life that
     has eluded them so far.

12   American survey. Cameron et al. 1989.

13   From a French national survey. Calculated from Hastings
     & Hastings 1987, p 500. See also Netting 1992.

14   We might add that society, because of its emphasis on
     immediate gratification, cannot compel young people to
     hold their sexual desires in abeyance for more than a de-
     cade of their lives, and yet, it cannot openly condone their
     promiscuity, due to the important economic role the 'nu-
     clear family' still holds in consumerist society. In this sce-
     nario, young people drift without direction, becoming

increasingly entangled in complex and ultimately injurious relationships.

15 U.S. Department of Commerce 1985, Table 7, p 141.

16 Knox 1985.

17 Downey 1990-91; Kandel et al. 1991. Intoxicants of the stronger variety, such as cocaine and drugs other than alcohol or cannabis, are particularly likely to increase despondency.

18 Chadwick & Heaton 1992, C3-6, p 98.

19 As with so many other things in the world, the route to marriage has become reduced to a well-ordered, scientific 'procedure' that nevertheless requires professional 'guidance'. Such unnecessary complexification makes marriage that much more threatening, and makes love that much more difficult to uncover. In this regard, see J.P. Decker, 'Wedding checklist: Couples add premarital counseling', *The Christian Science Monitor*, May 2, 1996, and M. Jordan, 'A short course on courting', *The Washington Post*, Feb 14, 1994.

20 See Sporer 2010B for research about the interaction effects of privacy, education, and media.

21 See Sporer 2010A; Sporer 2010B.

22 Many people also believe that the same total 'burden' applies to whatever sequence of choices a person makes, thus making the search for an easier life course futile. See

Sporer 2010B for extended discussions and research about the varied approaches to the 'timeline' issue.

23 Although education affects level of maturity, it also influences opinions and attitudes, which in turn can improve or degrade relationship quality. The higher the level of schooling, pre-marital courtship concerns, such as background, will be more congruous. Courtship and the beginning of the relationship will be stable if opinions on major issues are parallel, which often helps to create later placidity. However, opinions about matters after marriage will be varied, perhaps leading to less happiness in later married life. See Sporer 2010C for further discussions.

24 Diehl 1986. There is little research into the symbolism of mazes or labyrinths. Carl Jung referred to the subject only rarely in his extensive works. Yet, the maze must have considerable psychological power, considering that it was prominently used in Gothic cathedrals, with the largest example at Chartres. The perfect enclosure of the traditional maze, the unified system within well-established unchanging boundaries, gives one confidence, but only *if* one believes that it represents life. Perhaps the transformation inherent in the symbolism of the maze is an all too disturbing concept, now that the goal of life is not located at a detectable, unshifting centre, but somewhere outside. If there is anything that modern man desperately seeks, it is stability, and the maze, now a hated word in the post-Reformation interpretation, offers an articulation only of the pathological doubts that plague modern times.

References

Bar-Yam M., Kohlberg L., Naame A., 1980, Moral reasoning of students in different cultural, social, and educational settings, *American Journal of Education*, May 88(3), 345-362.

Boyes M.C., Allen SG, 1993, Styles of parent-child interaction and moral reasoning in adolescence, *Merrill Palmer Quarterly*, Oct 39(4), 551-570.

Cameron P., Cameron K., Proctor K., 1989, Effect of homosexuality upon public health and social order, *Psychological Reports*, 64, 1167-1179.

Chadwick B.A., Heaton T.B., 1992, eds, *Statistical Handbook on the American Family*, Oryx Press, Phoenix.

Christopher F.S., 1988, An initial investigation into a continuum of premarital sexual pressure, *Journal of Sex Research*, May 25(2), 255-266.

Diehl, H., 1986, Into the maze of the self: The Protestant transformation of the image of the labyrinth, *The Journal of Medieval and Renaissance Studies*, Fall 16(2), 281-301.

Downey A.M., 1990-1991, The impact of drug abuse upon adolescent suicide, *Omega*, 22(4), 261-275.

Eisenberg N., Miller P.A., Shell R., McNalley S., Shea C., 1991, Prosocial development in adolescence: A longitudinal study, *Developmental Psychology*, 27(5), 849-857.

Gordon M., Miller R.L., 1984, Going steady in the 1980s: Exclusive relationships in six Connecticut high schools, *Sociology and Social Research*, Jul 68(4), 463-479.

Hastings E.H., Hastings P.K., 1987, *Index to International Public Opinion, 1985-1986*, Greenwood Press, New York.

Kandel DB, Raveis VH, Davies M, 1991, Suicidal ideation in adolescence: Depression, substance use, and other risk factors, *Journal of Youth and Adolescence*, Apr 20(2), 289-310.

Knox D., 1985, Breaking up: The cover story versus the real story, *Free Inquiry in Creative Sociology*, 13(2), 131-132.

Muram D., Rosenthal T.L., Tolley E.A., Peeler M.M., et al., 1992, Teenage pregnancy: Dating and sexual attitudes, *Journal of Sex Education and Therapy*, Win 18(4), 264-276.

Netting N.S., 1992, Sexuality in youth culture: Identity and change, *Adolescence*, Win 27(108), 961-976.

Schab F., 1991, Schooling without learning: Thirty years of cheating in high school, *Adolescence*, 26(104), 839-847.

Speicher B., 1992, Adolescent moral judgment and perceptions of family interaction, *Journal of Family Psychology*, Dec 6(2), 128-138.

Sporer, P.D., 2010A, *Liberating Love*, Quenstedt Press, Chester.

Sporer, P.D., 2010B, *The Dimensions of Companionship*, Quenstedt Press, Chester.

Sporer, P.D., 2010C, *Equal but Different*, Quenstedt Press, Chester.

U.S. Department of Commerce, 1985, *1980 Census of the Population*, Volume 2 Subject Reports, Marital Characteristics, U.S. Government Printing Office, Washington, DC.

Weisheit R.A., Hopkins R.H., Kearney K.A., Mauss A.L., 1982, Substance abuse, nonconformity, and the inability to assign problem responsibility, *The Journal of Drug Issues*, Spr 12(2), 199-209.

Index

neglect, 88
negotiate, 84
noble, 74
number, 2, 7, 52, 54, 84

obligations, 2, 41, 54, 61, 80
obstacles, 24, 84
occupation, 33, 80, 84, 85, 99
opinions, 25, 34, 44, 45
opportunities, 4, 6, 53, 67, 69,
    72, 82, 84, 88
opposite sex, 8, 10, 15, 31, 34,
    43, 51, 59, 67, 71, 91, 104
order, 2, 5, 6, 9, 15, 16, 18, 24,
    29, 32, 40–42, 46, 60, 62,
    63, 74, 80, 83, 96, 100, 101
origin, 10, 56, 63, 67, 70, 82,
    87, 102
over-dependence, 51, 84

parameters, 11, 18
parents. *See* family
parenthood, 85
partners, 2, 3, 16, 31, 33, 35,
    43, 47, 48, 51–53, 59, 81–83,
    85, 90
paths, 36, 39, 47, 62, 85, 87,
    90, 96, 100
patriotism, 100

peace, 67
perceptions, 8, 25, 64, 69, 79
perfection, 4, 55, 100, 101, 105
period, 1, 5, 7, 10, 40, 52, 54,
    70, 91, 101
perseverance, 83
personality: emotions, 8, 27,
    68, 88; extroversion, 64;
    traits, 2, 17, 27, 28, 34, 80
perspective, 8, 11, 13, 29, 30,
    33, 83, 106
phenomenon, 33, 50
planning, 3, 60
plans, 18, 24, 28, 36, 48, 68,
    70, 72, 73, 86, 91, 107
political issues. *See* govern-
    ment and politics
popular, 48, 62, 101, 103, 106
possessions, 100, 104, 105
poverty. *See* financial issues
powerful, 5, 30, 60, 66, 86, 97
pragmaticism, 11, 12, 25, 48,
    49, 89
pre-marital relations: attrac-
    tiveness, 8, 25–27, 29, 33,
    36, 41, 45, 49; cohabitation,
    54; commitment, 2, 3, 34,
    46, 55, 56, 59, 63, 72; court-
    ship, 17, 40, 51, 52, 88; dat-

ing, 15, 16, 18, 24, 31, 33, 35,
36, 40–46, 48, 50–52, 72, 88;
opposite sex, 8, 10, 15, 31,
34, 43, 51, 59, 67, 71, 91, 104
prejudice, 16, 62
principles, 5, 6, 9, 10, 14, 16,
17, 24, 29, 35, 53, 59, 64, 68,
84, 85, 89, 91, 95, 96, 107
private, 54, 67, 68
processes, 10, 12, 14, 23, 32, 35,
64, 98
profound, 17, 51, 100
progress, 4, 8, 46, 80, 84, 106
promises, 2, 104
protection, 26, 50, 51, 61, 70
Protestantism, 101
pro-social, 25, 42, 68
psychological, 1, 2, 7, 9, 12, 28,
39, 66, 67, 81, 86, 91
puberty, 10, 44, 47
public, 2, 33, 105
pursuit, 36, 56, 62, 63, 68, 82

quality, 26, 66, 68, 80, 89, 97
question, 11, 13, 15, 18, 19, 29,
32, 37, 49, 52, 53, 72, 74, 86
quid pro quo, 103

race, 1, 45

rank. *See* status
rational, 32, 70
reason, 2, 19, 46, 50, 51, 72, 81,
82, 102
reasoning, 9, 11–16, 19, 35, 42,
45, 50, 54, 55, 60, 68, 89,
106
recreation, 71
reflection, 3, 101
reinforcement, 36
relationship: companionate, 9,
18, 90; dating, 15, 16, 50;
intimate, 4, 6, 17, 24, 33, 36,
40, 48, 49, 69, 83, 95, 103;
love, 3, 26; male-female, 16,
17, 25, 47; marital, 4, 17, 55,
99; proper, 12; relationship
ideals, 12; satisfying relationship, 9; type of, 3, 40;
unique, 5
reliance, 6, 10, 15, 23–25, 31,
84
religion: churches, 53–55, 100,
101; general, 63; Jesus
Christ, 101; Protestantism,
101; Roman Catholic, 101
representations, 9, 54, 61, 103
resistance, 6, 105
respect, 3, 4, 13, 42, 107

www.ingramcontent.com/pod-product-compliance
Lightning Source LLC
Chambersburg PA
CBHW031210270326
41931CB00006B/497